ECONOMIC ISSUES, PROBLEMS AND PERSPECTIVES

UNEMPLOYMENT: A CLOSER LOOK

ECONOMIC ISSUES, PROBLEMS AND PERSPECTIVES

Additional books in this series can be found on Nova's website under the Series tab.

Additional E-books in this series can be found on Nova's website under the E-books tab.

ECONOMIC ISSUES, PROBLEMS AND PERSPECTIVES

UNEMPLOYMENT: A CLOSER LOOK

JACOB S. MLAKAR
EDITOR

Nova Science Publishers, Inc.
New York

For permission to use material from this book please contact us:
Telephone 631-231-7269; Fax 631-231-8175
Web Site: http://www.novapublishers.com

Additional color graphics may be available in the e-book version of this book.

LIBRARY OF CONGRESS CATALOGING-IN-PUBLICATION DATA
Unemployment : a closer look / editor, Jacob S. Mlakar.
p. cm.
Includes index.
ISBN 978-1-61122-762-8 (hbk.)
1. Unemployment--United States. 2. Unemployed--United States. 3. Unemployment insurance--United States. I. Mlakar, Jacob S.
HD5724.U594 2010
331.13'7973--dc22
2010043926

Published by Nova Science Publishers, Inc. † New York

CONTENTS

Preface		**vii**
Chapter 1	Unemployment Insurance: Available Unemployment Benefits and Legislative Activity *Katelin P. Isaacs, Julie M. Whittaker and Alison M. Shelton*	**1**
Chapter 2	Unemployment: Issues and Policies *Jane G. Gravelle, Thomas L. Hungerford and Marc Labonte*	**45**
Chapter 3	Unemployment Compensation (UC) and the Unemployment Trust Fund (UTF): Funding UC Benefits *Julie M. Whittaker*	**69**
Chapter 4	Unemployment Compensation (Insurance) and Military Service *Julie M. Whittaker*	**79**
Chapter 5	Does Unemployment Insurance Inhibit Job Search? *Carolyn Maloney*	**87**
Chapter 6	Understanding the Economy: Working Mothers in the Great Recession *Carolyn Maloney*	**93**

Chapter 7	Women in the Recession: Working Mothers Face High Rates of Unemployment *Carolyn B. Maloney and Charles E. Schumer*	**99**
Chapter 8	Understanding the Economy: Long-Term Unemployment in the African American Community *Carolyn B. Maloney*	**109**
Chapter 9	Understanding the Economy: Unemployment in the Hispanic Community *Carolyn B. Maloney*	**121**
Chapter 10	Understanding the Economy: Unemployment among Young Workers *Carolyn B. Maloney*	**137**
Chapter 11	Extending Unemployment Insurance Benefits: The Cost of Inaction for Disabled Workers *Carolyn B. Maloney and Charles E. Schumer*	**151**

Chapter Sources **157**

Index **159**

PREFACE

The National Bureau of Economic Research (NBER) has declared the U.S. economy to be in recession since December 2007. In response to high unemployment, some members of Congress proposed job creation bills, following several policy steps taken since the economy entered the recession, including stimulus bills in 2008 and 2009, an unprecedented expansion in direct assistance to the financial sector by the Federal Reserve, and the Troubled Asset Relief Program (TARP). This book discusses the current unemployment outlook and analyzes policy proposals to address the issues and options for financing proposals.

Chapter 1- Various benefits may be available to unemployed workers to provide income support. When eligible workers lose their jobs, the Unemployment Compensation (UC) program may provide up to 26 weeks of income support through the payment of regular UC benefits. Unemployment benefits may be extended for up to 53 weeks by the temporarily authorized Emergency Unemployment Compensation (EUC08) program and extended for up to a further 13 or 20 weeks by the permanent Extended Benefit (EB) program under certain state economic conditions. Certain groups of workers who lose their jobs because of international competition may qualify for income support through Trade Adjustment Act (TAA) programs. Unemployed workers may be eligible to receive Disaster Unemployment Assistance (DUA) benefits if they are not eligible for regular UC and if their unemployment may be directly attributed to a declared major disaster.

Chapter 2- The National Bureau of Economic Research (NBER) has declared the U.S. economy to be in recession since December 2007. The unemployment rate in December 2007 was 4.9%; by October 2009, the unemployment rate was above 10%. Although economic output began to grow in the third quarter of 2009, as expected the labor market remained weak into 2010. In response to high unemployment, some Members of Congress proposed job creation bills, following several policy steps taken since the economy entered the recession, including stimulus bills in 2008 (P.L. 110-185) and 2009 (P.L. 111-5), an unprecedented expansion in direct assistance to the financial sector by the Federal Reserve, and the Troubled Asset Relief Program (TARP; P.L. 110-343).

Chapter 3- The National Bureau of Economic Research (NBER) has declared the U.S. economy to be in recession since December 2007. The unemployment rate in December 2007 was 4.9%; by October 2009, the unemployment rate was above 10%. Although economic output began to grow in the third quarter of 2009, as expected the labor market remained weak into 2010. In response to high unemployment, some Members of Congress proposed job creation bills, following several policy steps taken since the economy entered the recession, including stimulus bills in 2008 (P.L. 110-185) and 2009 (P.L. 111-5), an unprecedented expansion in direct assistance to the financial sector by the Federal Reserve, and the Troubled Asset Relief Program (TARP; P.L. 110-343).

Chapter 4- The Unemployment Compensation (UC) program contains several provisions relevant to current and former military service personnel and their families. The UC program does not provide benefits for military servicemembers on active duty. However, former active duty military personnel (and certain reservists) separated from active duty may be eligible for Unemployment Compensation for Ex-Servicemembers (UCX).

Spouses of military service personnel who voluntarily quit a job to accompany their spouses on account of a military transfer may be eligible for UC benefits, based on the laws of the state where the civilian spouse was employed.

Chapter 5- The Unemployment Compensation (UC) program contains several provisions relevant to current and former military service personnel and their families. The UC program does not provide benefits for military servicemembers on active duty. However, former active duty military personnel (and certain reservists) separated from active duty may be eligible for Unemployment Compensation for Ex-Servicemembers (UCX).

Spouses of military service personnel who voluntarily quit a job to accompany their spouses on account of a military transfer may be eligible for UC benefits, based on the laws of the state where the civilian spouse was employed.

Chapter 6- The Great Recession has taken a huge toll on working families. The vast majority of jobs lost were lost by men, but a substantial number of jobs were lost by women during this recession. From December 2007 to April 2010, women lost 46 jobs for every 100 jobs lost by men.[1] By comparison, during the 2001 recession, women lost 17 jobs for every 100 lost by men and women lost less than 2 jobs for every 100 jobs lost by men during the 1990s recession. Indeed, in recent months, women lost jobs while men gained jobs.[2] From October 2009 to March 2010, women lost 22,000 jobs while men gained 260,000.[3] Women's increased vulnerability to the business cycle has important repercussions for families' economic security. This report provides an updated look at the employment situation of working mothers[4] with children under 18 years old, and examines the impact of the recession on their participation in the labor market using unpublished data from the Bureau of Labor Statistics.[5]

Chapter 7- Working women have received pink slips in growing numbers over the course of the current recession, which began in December 2007. For the first 3 months of the recession, when job losses were relatively light, women actually gained rather than lost jobs. This uptick in women's employment is similar to what has happened in previous recessions. However, in August 2008, this recession began to look quite different from past downturns. Women's job losses picked up pace to become a significant fraction of the total monthly job losses.

Chapter 8- This report provides an in-depth look at unemployment, including long-term unemployment, among African American or black workers. Since 1972, when the Bureau of Labor Statistics started tracking unemployment rates by race, it has become clear that the overall unemployment rate for the United States has masked the depth of the unemployment problem within the African American community.

Chapter 9- Workers across the United States have been hard hit during the "Great Recession," but in many respects, workers of Latino or Hispanic ethnicity are facing even greater employment challenges.[1] Latinos make up over one-seventh (14.8 percent) of the U.S. labor force, but represented almost one- fifth (19.0 percent) of the unemployed in March 2010.

Rising unemployment in the Latino community appears to be caused in large part by the bursting of the housing bubble. Employment in the construction sector reached a peak of 7.7 million workers in August 2006. By February 2010, however, employment had plummeted to 5.6 million workers - a 27.8 percent drop. As this report shows, Latino workers are over-represented in the sectors that contracted the most during the recession, including the construction industry.

Chapter 10- Although the economy has gained strength and overall labor market conditions have improved in recent months, younger workers have continued to struggle finding work. Employers added over half a million jobs in the last four months, yet the unemployment rate for young workers reached a record 19.6 percent in April 2010, the highest level for this age group since the Bureau of Labor Statistics began tracking unemployment in 1947.

Historically, young workers (ages 16 to 24) face considerably higher unemployment rates than prime- age workers (ages 25 to 54). Even before the recession began, one out of every eight young workers was unemployed, a rate of unemployment more than two and a half times that of prime-age workers. While the gap narrowed during the recession, young workers saw their unemployment rate climb steadily and still have a significantly higher unemployment rate than prime-age and older workers.

Chapter 11- The Great Recession left a battered labor market in its wake. The unprecedented rise in longterm unemployment is particularly troubling.[1] Many of the long-term unemployed have continued to receive much-needed support thanks to Congress and the Administration's expansion and extension of the unemployment insurance benefits program. However, these crucial programs are scheduled to expire next—month. The expiration of the unemployment insurance benefits extension puts millions of out-of-work Americans and their families at risk of real economic hardship. This brief provides an overview of the economic impact of extending unemployment benefits insurance, including a new estimate of the cost of inaction.

In: Unemployment: A Closer Look
Editors: Jacob S. Mlakar ISBN: 978-1-61122-762-8

Chapter 1

UNEMPLOYMENT INSURANCE: AVAILABLE UNEMPLOYMENT BENEFITS AND LEGISLATIVE ACTIVITY

Katelin P. Isaacs, Julie M. Whittaker and Alison M. Shelton

SUMMARY

Various benefits may be available to unemployed workers to provide income support. When eligible workers lose their jobs, the Unemployment Compensation (UC) program may provide up to 26 weeks of income support through the payment of regular UC benefits. Unemployment benefits may be extended for up to 53 weeks by the temporarily authorized Emergency Unemployment Compensation (EUC08) program and extended for up to a further 13 or 20 weeks by the permanent Extended Benefit (EB) program under certain state economic conditions. Certain groups of workers who lose their jobs because of international competition may qualify for income support through Trade Adjustment Act (TAA) programs. Unemployed workers may be eligible to receive Disaster Unemployment Assistance (DUA) benefits if they are not eligible for regular UC and if their unemployment may be directly attributed to a declared major disaster.

The authorization for the EUC08 program expires on November 30, 2010. Those beneficiaries receiving tier I, II, III, or IV EUC08 benefits before

November 27, 2010, are "grandfathered" for their remaining weeks of eligibility for that particular tier only. There will be no new entrants into any tier of the EUC08 program after November 27, 2010. See the section in this report on "Policy Proposals that Target Unemployment Benefit Exhaustees" for additional measures to address the needs of the long-term unemployed.

The American Recovery and Reinvestment Act of 2009 (ARRA), P.L. 111-5, contained several provisions affecting unemployment benefits. ARRA temporarily increased benefits by $25 per week (Federal Additional Compensation, or FAC); extended the EUC08 program through 2009; temporarily provided for 100% federal financing of EB; and allowed states the option of temporarily easing EB eligibility requirements. ARRA also suspended income taxation on the first $2,400 of unemployment benefits received in 2009. In addition, states do not owe or accrue interest, through December 2010, on federal loans to states for the payment of unemployment benefits. ARRA also provided for a special transfer of up to $7 billion in federal monies to state unemployment programs as "incentive payments" for changing certain state UC laws as well as transferred $500 million to the states for administering unemployment programs. P.L. 111-92 expanded the number of weeks available in the EUC08 program through the creation of two additional tiers. P.L. 111-118 and P.L. 111-144 extended the EUC08 program, 100% federal financing of EB, and the FAC through the end of February 2010 and April 5, 2010, respectively. P.L. 111-157 extended these three UC provisions through the week ending on or before June 2, 2010.

On July 22, 2010, the President signed P.L. 111-205, the Unemployment Compensation Extension Act of 2010, into law. P.L. 111-205 extends the availability of EUC08 and 100% federal financing of EB until November 30, 2010. P.L. 111-205 does not, however, extend the authorization for the $25 FAC benefit, which expired on May 29, 2010 (May 30, 2010, in New York state).

INTRODUCTION

A variety of benefits may be available to unemployed workers to provide them with income support during a spell of unemployment. The cornerstone of this income support is the joint federal-state Unemployment Compensation (UC) program, which may provide income support through the payment of UC benefits for up to a maximum of 26 weeks.[1] Other programs that may provide workers with income support are more specialized. They may target special groups of workers, be automatically triggered by certain economic conditions, be temporarily created by Congress with a set expiration date, or target typically ineligible workers through a disaster declaration.

UC benefits may be extended at the state level by the permanent Extended Benefit (EB) program if high unemployment exists within the state. Once regular unemployment benefits are exhausted, the EB program may provide up to an additional 13 or 20 weeks of benefits, depending on worker eligibility, state law, and economic conditions in the state. The EB program is funded 50% by the federal government and 50% by the states, although the 2009 stimulus package (P.L. 111-5, as amended) temporarily provides for 100% federal funding of the EB program.

A temporary unemployment insurance program, the Emergency Unemployment Compensation (EUC08) program, began in July 2008. The authorization for the EUC08 program expires on November 30, 2010. Those beneficiaries receiving tier I, II, III, or IV EUC08 benefits before November 27, 2010 (November 28, 2010, in New York), are "grandfathered" for their remaining weeks of eligibility for that particular tier only. There will be no new entrants into any tier of the EUC08 program after November 27, 2010. If an individual is eligible to continue to receive his or her remaining EUC08 tier I benefit after November 27, 2010, that individual will not be entitled to tier II benefits once those tier I benefits are exhausted. This was the eighth time Congress has created a federal temporary program that has extended unemployment compensation during an economic slowdown.[2] The EUC08 benefit is 100% federally funded. State UC agencies administer the EUC08 benefit along with regular UC benefits. See **Appendix A** for a diagram of the various unemployment benefits available to workers.

If an unemployed worker is not eligible to receive UC benefits and the worker's unemployment may be directly attributed to a declared major disaster, a worker may be eligible to receive Disaster Unemployment Assistance (DUA) benefits. The disaster declaration will include information on whether DUA benefits are available. For information on Disaster Unemployment Assistance, see CRS Report RS22022, *Disaster Unemployment Assistance (DUA)*, by Julie M. Whittaker and Alison M. Shelton.

Certain groups of workers who lose their jobs because of international competition may qualify for additional or supplemental support through Trade Adjustment Act (TAA) programs or (for certain workers aged 50 or older) through Reemployment Trade Adjustment Assistance (RTAA). This report does not describe the TAA or RTAA programs. (Please see CRS Report RS22718, *Trade Adjustment Assistance for Workers (TAA) and Reemployment Trade Adjustment Assistance (RTAA)*, by John J. Topoleski, for information on these programs.)

This report describes four kinds of unemployment benefits: regular UC, EB, EUC08, and DUA. The report explains their basic eligibility requirements, benefits, and financing structure.

UNEMPLOYMENT COMPENSATION

UC is a joint federal-state program financed by federal taxes under the Federal Unemployment Tax Act (FUTA) and by state payroll taxes under the State Unemployment Tax Acts (SUTA). The UC program has a direct impact on almost every business in the United States as most businesses are subject to state and federal unemployment taxes. An estimated $6.0 billion in federal unemployment taxes and $44.9 billion in state unemployment taxes will be collected in FY20 10. In FY20 10, states will spend an estimated $66.7 billion on regular UC benefits and the state share of the EB program. The federal government will spend additional amounts described in section "Appropriation and Outlays" below. Approximately 131.7 million jobs are covered by the UC program. At the end of the week of April 10, 2010, 5.0 million unemployed workers received UC. The average weekly UC benefit was $307 in June 2010 (and this amount is supplemented by the $25 weekly Federal Additional Compensation, or FAC, program payment for workers who were receiving UC benefits before May 29, 2010; see section on "Federal Additional Compensation" below for more details on FAC expiration and "grandfathering").

Originally, the intent of the UC program, among other things, was to help counter economic fluctuations such as recessions.[3] This intent is reflected in the current UC program's funding and benefit structure. When the economy grows, UC program revenue rises through increased tax revenues while UC program spending falls as fewer workers are unemployed. The effect of collecting more taxes than are spent dampens demand in the economy. This also creates a surplus of funds or a "cushion" of available funds for the UC program to draw upon during a recession. In a recession, UC tax revenue falls and UC program spending rises as more workers lose their jobs and receive UC benefits. The increased amount of UC payments to unemployed workers dampens the economic effect of earnings losses by injecting additional funds into the economy.

Authorization

The underlying framework of the UC system is contained in the Social Security Act (the Act). Title III of the Act authorizes grants to states for the administration of state UC laws, Title IX authorizes the various components of the federal Unemployment Trust Fund (UTF), and Title XII authorizes advances or loans to insolvent state UC programs.

Appropriation and Outlays

The federal government appropriates funds for federal and state UC program administration, the federal share of EB payments, the EUC08 program, and federal loans to insolvent state UC programs. In FY2009, states received $4.32 billion from the federal government for the administration of their UC programs, $4.12 billion for the federal share of EB payments, and $32.66 billion for the temporary, federally financed EUC08 program. In FY20 10, a preliminary estimate (which does not include the extensions of EUC08 and 100% federal financing of the EB program after February 2010) is that the states will receive an estimated $5.87 billion from the federal government for the administration of their UC programs, $10.5 billion for the federal share of EB payments, and $43.57 billion for the temporary EUC08 program.

Administration

The U.S. Department of Labor (DOL) administers the federal portion of the UC system, which operates in each state, the District of Columbia, Puerto Rico, and the Virgin Islands. Federal law sets broad rules that the 53 state programs must follow. These include the broad categories of workers that must be covered by the program, the method for triggering the EB and EUC08 programs, the floor on the highest state unemployment tax rate to be imposed on employers (5.4%), and how the states will repay UTF loans. If the states do not follow these rules, their employers may lose a portion of their state unemployment tax credit when their federal income tax is calculated. The federal tax pays for both federal and state administrative costs, the federal share of the EB program, the EUC08 program, loans to insolvent state UC accounts, and state employment services. The 2009 stimulus package provided a total of $500 million in additional funds to states to help with administrative costs of the regular UC program, the EB program, and the EUC08 program.

Eligibility for Regular Unemployment Compensation

Broad Federal Guidelines Result in Different State Requirements

Whereas federal laws and regulations provide broad guidelines on UC benefit coverage, eligibility, and benefit determination, the specifics of regular UC benefits are determined by each state. This results in essentially 53 different programs. States determine UC benefit eligibility, payments, and duration through state laws and program regulations. Generally, UC eligibility is based on attaining qualified wages and employment in covered work over a 12-month period (called a base period) prior to unemployment.

Base Period

The base period is the time period during which wages earned or hours/weeks worked are examined to determine a worker's monetary entitlement to UC. Almost all states use the first four of the last five completed calendar quarters preceding the filing of the claim as their base period. This may result in a lag of up to five months between the end of the base period and the date a worker becomes unemployed. As a result there are some instances when workers with substantial labor market attachment are ineligible for UC benefits. In particular, recent entrants to the workforce, or re-entrants, may be ineligible under this definition. Federal law allows states to develop expanded definitions of the base period.

A list of states' base periods can be found at *http://www.workforcesecurity.doleta.gov/unemploy/* pdf/uilawcompar/20 1 0/monetary.pdf, Table 3-2.

Alternative Base Period

Almost two-thirds of states allow the use of an alternative base period (ABP) for workers failing to qualify under the regular base period. For example, if the worker fails to qualify using wages and employment in the first four of the last five completed calendar quarters, then the state might use wages and employment in the last four completed calendar quarters.

Extended Base Period

Several states allow workers who have no wages in the current base period to use older wages and employment under certain conditions. These conditions typically involve illness or injury. For example, a worker who was injured on the job and who has collected workers' compensation benefits may use wages and employment preceding the date of the worker's injury to establish eligibility.

Base Period Provisions in the 2009 Stimulus Package

The 2009 stimulus package (P.L. 111-5) provided up to $7 billion to states as an incentive to make changes to their unemployment programs. As of May 5, 2010, $2.8 billion of this fund had been distributed to states. One-third of a state's share of this amount is contingent on state law allowing use of a base period that includes the most recently completed calendar quarter before the start of the benefit year for the purpose of determining UC eligibility. The remaining two-thirds of a state's share of the $7 billion is contingent on qualifying for the first one-third payment (by adopting an alternative base period definition), plus adopting two of four additional provisions (described in section "2009 Stimulus Provisions Relating to Regular Unemployment Compensation" below).[4]

Qualifying Wages or Employment

All states require a worker to have earned a certain amount of wages or to have worked for a certain period of time (or both) within the base period to be monetarily eligible to receive any UC benefits. The methods that states use to determine monetary eligibility vary greatly.

Multiple of High-Quarter Wages. Under this method, workers must earn a certain dollar amount in the quarter with the highest earnings of their base period. Workers must also earn total base- period wages that are a multiple—typically 1 .5—of the high-quarter wages. For example, if a worker earns $5,000 in the high quarter, the worker must earn at least another $2,500 in the rest of the base period. States require earnings in more than one quarter to minimize the likelihood that workers with high earnings in only one quarter receive benefits. Although the worker might be monetarily eligible through the earnings accrued in one quarter, these "multiple of high quarter wages" states do not deem those workers to be substantially attached to the labor market.

Multiple of Weekly Benefit Amount. Under this method, the state first computes the worker's weekly benefit amount. The worker must have earned a multiple—often 40—of this amount during the base period. For example, if a worker's weekly benefit amount equals $100, then the worker will need base period earnings of 40 times $100, or $4,000, before any UC would be paid. Most states also require wages in at least two quarters. Some states have weighted schedules that require varying multiples for varying weekly benefits.

Flat Qualifying Amount. States using this method require a certain dollar amount of total wages to be earned during the base period. This method is used by most states with an annual-wage requirement for determining the weekly benefit and by some states with a high-quarter wage/weekly benefit requirement.

Weeks/Hours of Employment. Under this method, the worker must have worked a certain number of weeks/hours at a certain weekly/hourly wage.

2009 Stimulus Provisions Relating to Regular Unemployment Compensation

The American Recovery and Reinvestment Act of 2009 (P.L. 111-5, the 2009 stimulus package), as amended, provides for a supplementary benefit payment of $25 per week for unemployment compensation programs (regular UC, EB, EUC, TAA and DUA) through May 29, 2010. The supplemental $25 weekly benefit is grandfathered for individuals who have not exhausted benefits before May 29, 2010, although no supplementary compensation is payable for any week beginning after December 11, 2010 (see section on "Federal Additional Compensation" below for more details on FAC expiration and "grandfathering"). States are not be allowed to alter the method of computing unemployment compensation in such a manner that the weekly benefit amount would be less than the benefit amount that would have been payable under state law as of December 31, 2008. The $25 weekly additional benefit is financed by the federal government through general revenues.

The stimulus package also provided up to $7 billion to states as an incentive to make changes to their unemployment programs. One-third of this amount is contingent on states allowing use of a base period that includes the most recently completed calendar quarter before the start of the benefit year for the purpose of determining UC eligibility. The remaining two-thirds of a state's share of the $7 billion is contingent on the state qualifying for the first one-third payment, and state law containing at least two of four additional provisions. These additional provisions include:

1. making unemployment compensation available to workers seeking part-time work;
2. making unemployment compensation available to individuals who quit their jobs voluntarily for compelling family reasons (domestic violence, illness or disability of an immediate family member, spouse relocating for a new job);
3. providing at least 26 additional weeks of unemployment benefits to workers who have exhausted all rights to regular benefits but are enrolled and making satisfactory progress in a state-approved training program or in a job training program authorized under the Workforce investment Act of 1998; and
4. providing dependents' allowances to all individuals with a dependent at a level equal to at least $15 per dependent per week.

Table 1. State Unemployment Compensation Benefits Amounts, January 2010 (in Dollars)

	Minimum Weekly UC Benefit Amount	Minimum If Dependents' Allowance[a]	Maximum Weekly UC Benefit Amount[b]	Maximum If Dependents' Allowance[a]
Alabama	45		265	
Alaska	56	128	370	442
Arizona	60		240	
Arkansas	79		441	
California	40		450	
Colorado	25		443	487
Connecticut	15	30	537	612
Delaware	20		330	

Table 1. (Continued)

	Minimum Weekly UC Benefit Amount	Minimum If Dependents' Allowance[a]	Maximum Weekly UC Benefit Amount[b]	Maximum If Dependents' Allowance[a]
District of Columbia	50		359	
Florida	32		275	
Georgia	44		330	
Hawaii	5		559	
Idaho	72		334	
Illinois	51	77	385	531
Indiana	50		390	
Iowa	56	67	374	459
Kansas	109		436	
Kentucky	39		415	
Louisiana	10		247	
Maine	62	93	356	534
Maryland	25	65	410	943
Massachusetts	33	49	629	
Michigan	117	147	362	585
Minnesota	38		377	
Mississippi	30		235	
Missouri	35		320	
Montana	125		422	
Nebraska	30		318	
Nevada	16		400	
New Hampshire	32	100	427	526
New Jersey	87	106.50	600	
New Mexico	71		426	
New York	64		405	
North Carolina	43		505	
North Dakota	43		431	
Ohio	106		375	503
Oklahoma	16		430	
Oregon	115		493	572
Pennsylvania	35	43	564	682
Rhode Island	68	118	546	

Table 1. (Continued)

	Minimum Weekly UC Benefit Amount	Minimum If Dependents' Allowance[a]	Maximum Weekly UC Benefit Amount[b]	Maximum If Dependents' Allowance[a]
South Carolina	20		326	
South Dakota	28		309	
Tennessee	30		275	
Texas	59		406	
Utah	29		451	
Vermont	64		425	
Virginia	54		378	
Washington	133		560	
West Virginia	24		424	
Wisconsin	54		363	
Wyoming	31		438	

Source: Congressional Research Service (CRS) table compiled from *Significant Provisions of State Unemployment Insurance Laws, January 2010*, U.S. Department of Labor, Employment and Training Administration, at *http://www.workforcesecurity.doleta.gov/unemploy/content/sigpros/2010-2019/January2010.pdf.*

a. The figures for minimum and maximum benefits include dependents' allowances for the maximum number of dependents.

b. If a state has dependents' allowances and only one amount is given, the maximum is the same with or without the allowance.

Data Collection Considerations

The wide variation seen in state UC program laws and regulations also exists among the states' data collections. All states collect information on earnings by quarter for each worker. A handful of states collect information on the number of weeks worked during the base period. Even fewer states collect information on the numbers of hours worked during a quarter. As a result, most states use information on quarters worked, quarterly earnings, and cumulative earnings in determining eligibility and the amount of benefit.[5] It does not appear that any state measures both hours of work and weeks of work in the base period.

Determination and Duration of Regular Unemployment Compensation

Generally, benefits are based on wages for covered work over a 12-month period (the "base period" or "alternative base period," described above). Most state benefit formulas replace half of a claimant's average weekly wage up to a weekly maximum. All states disregard some earnings during unemployment as an incentive to take short-term or part-time work while searching for a permanent position. Generally, the worker's UC payment equals the difference between the weekly benefit amount and earnings.

Table 1 lists the minimum and maximum UC benefits for each state.[6] Weekly maximums in January 2010 ranged from $235 (Mississippi) to $629 (Massachusetts) and, in states that provide dependents' allowances, up to $943 (Massachusetts). In March 2010, the average weekly benefit was $310 (and this amount is supplemented by the $25 weekly FAC program payment for individuals receiving benefits prior to May 29, 2010; see section on "Federal Additional Compensation" below for more details on FAC expiration and "grandfathering"). Benefits are available for up to 26 weeks (28 weeks in Montana and 30 weeks in Massachusetts). The average regular UC benefit duration in December 2009 was 19 weeks. In April 2010, approximately 5.0 million unemployed workers received regular state UC benefits in a given week.

UC Benefit Financing: Unemployment Taxes on Employers

UC benefits are financed through employer taxes.[7] The federal taxes on employers are under the authority of the Federal Unemployment Tax Act (FUTA), and the state taxes are under the authority given by the State Unemployment Tax Acts (SUTA). These taxes are deposited in the appropriate accounts within the Unemployment Trust Fund (UTF).

Federal Unemployment Tax Act

The net FUTA tax rate on employers in states with UC programs that are in compliance with all federal rules is 0.8% on the first $7,000 of each worker's earnings. The FUTA tax rate for employers is 6.2% on the first $7,000 of each worker's earnings, but a 5.4% credit against the federal FUTA tax is available to employers in states with complying UC programs, bringing the net FUTA tax down to 0.8%. (In tax year 2009, Michigan employers were required to pay a net FUTA tax of 1.1% because of outstanding federal loans to their state's UTF account.) The 0.8% FUTA tax funds both federal and state administrative costs as well as the federal share of the EB program, loans to insolvent state UC accounts, and state employment services. Federal law defines which jobs a state UC program must cover, provides rules concerning state borrowing from the UTF, and provides broad guidelines concerning benefit eligibility, in order for the state's employers to avoid paying the maximum FUTA tax rate (6.2%) on the first $7,000 of each employee's annual pay.

Federal law requires that a state must cover jobs in firms that pay at least $1,500 in wages during any calendar quarter or employ at least one worker in each of 20 weeks in the current or prior year. The FUTA tax is not paid by government or nonprofit employers, but state programs must cover government workers and all workers in nonprofits that employ at least four workers in each of 20 weeks in the current or prior year.[8]

Approximately $6.7 billion in FUTA taxes were collected in FY2009. The net balance in the federal accounts of the UTF (the Employment Security Administration Account, the Extended Unemployment Compensation Account for the EB and EUC08 programs, and the Federal Unemployment Account for federal loans to the states) on February 1, 2010, was approximately $6.0 billion. This figure includes $28 billion in general revenue advances to the UTF as of February 1, 2010, "incentive monies" for states to modernize their UC programs under the American Recovery and Reinvestment Act of 2009 (ARRA; P.L. 111-5), and is net of payments to state accounts for administrative expenses and UTF lending to state accounts for the payment of UC benefits.

Congress first passed a temporary FUTA surtax in 1976, and since 1983 the surtax has been applied in its current form (0.2% on the first $7,000 of employee wages). P.L. 111-92 extended the authorization of the FUTA surtax through June 2011.

ARRA Temporary Changes Federal Financing of Unemployment Benefits

ARRA (P.L. 111-5) made several important, albeit temporary, changes to the federal role in financing unemployment benefit programs. Under ARRA (as amended), the federal government temporarily uses UTF monies to finance 100% of EB payments through November 30, 2010 (under permanent law EB payments are financed 50% by the federal government and 50% by states).

The federal government also used UTF funds to finance a $500 million transfer to states for administering unemployment programs, and uses UTF funds for the $7 billion in incentive monies to states for undertaking modernization of their unemployment programs. ARRA also changed the financing of the EUC08 program, which from its implementation in July 2008 had been financed from the UTF, but starting with enactment of ARRA (on February 17, 2009) has been financed from general revenues of the Treasury. States continue to finance regular UC through SUTA revenues.

Table 2. State Unemployment Taxes: Taxable Wage Base and Rates, January 2010

State	Wages Subject to Tax ($)	Minimum State Unemployment Tax (%)[a]	Maximum State Unemployment Tax (%)[a]
Alabama	8,000	0.44	6.04
Alaska	34,100	1.00	5.40
Arizona	7,000	0.02	5.40
Arkansas	12,000	0.90	6.80
California	7,000	1.50	6.20
Colorado	10,000	0.00	5.40
Connecticut	15,000	1.90	6.80
Delaware	10,500	0.10	8.00
DC	9,000	1.30	6.60
Florida	7,000	0.12	5.40
Georgia	8,500	0.03	5.40
Hawaii	38,800	0.00	5.40
Idaho	33,200	0.45	5.40
Illinois	12,520	0.60	6.80
Indiana	9,500	1.10	5.60
Iowa	24,500	0.00	8.00
Kansas	8,000	0.00	7.40
Kentucky	8,000	1.00	10.00
Louisiana	7,700	0.10	6.20
Maine	12,000	0.44	5.40
Maryland	8,500	0.60	9.00
Massachusetts	14,000	1.26	12.27
Michigan	9,000	0.60	10.30

Table 2. (Continued)

State	Wages Subject to Tax ($)	Minimum State Unemployment Tax (%)[a]	Maximum State Unemployment Tax (%)[a]
Minnesota	27,000	0.56	10.70
Mississippi	7,000	0.70	5.40
Missouri	13,000	0.00	9.75
Montana	26,000	0.00	6.12
Nebraska	9,000	0.00	5.40
Nevada	27,000	0.25	5.40
New Hampshire	10,000	0.10	6.50
New Jersey	29,700	0.30	5.40
New Mexico	20,800	0.03	5.40
New York	8,500	0.70	8.70
North Carolina	19,700	0.00	6.84
North Dakota	24,700	0.20	9.86
Ohio	9,000	0.30	9.00
Oklahoma	14,900	0.10	5.50
Oregon	32,100	0.90	5.40
Pennsylvania	8,000	1.84	13.16
Rhode Island	19,000	1.69	9.79
South Carolina	7,000	1.14	6.00
South Dakota	10,000	0.00	8.50
Tennessee	9,000	0.50	10.00
Texas	9,000	0.26	6.26
Utah	28,300	0.20	9.20
Vermont	10,000	0.80	6.50
Virginia	8,000	0.18	6.28
Washington	36,800	0.00	5.40
West Virginia	12,000	1.50	7.50
Wisconsin	12,000	0.00	8.50
Wyoming	22,800	0.30	9.10

Source: CRS table compiled from *Significant Provisions of State Unemployment Insurance Laws, January 2010*, U.S. Department of Labor, Employment and Training Administration, at http://www.workforcesecurity.doleta.gov/ unemploy /content/sigpros/20 10-201 9/January20 10.pdf.

a. Tax rates apply only to experience-rated employers; states apply different rates to new employers.

State Unemployment Tax Acts

States levy their own payroll taxes (SUTA taxes) on employers to fund regular UC benefits and the state share of the EB program. The state unemployment tax rate on an employer is "experience rated" in all states, that is, the SUTA rate is based on the amount of UC paid to former employees. Generally, the more UC benefits paid to its former employees, the higher the tax rate of the employer, up to a maximum established by state law. The experience rating is intended to ensure an equitable distribution of UC program taxes among employers in relationship to their use of the UC program, and to encourage a stable workforce. State ceilings on taxable wages in January 2010 ranged from the $7,000 FUTA federal ceiling (eight states) to $38,900 (Hawaii). The minimum SUTA rates ranged from 0% (11 states) to 1.84% (Pennsylvania) in January 2010. Maximum SUTA rates ranged from 5.4% (15 states) to 13.16% (Pennsylvania) in January 2010. Approximately $31.1 billion in SUTA taxes were collected in FY2009.

State UC revenue is deposited in the U.S. Treasury. These deposits are counted as federal revenue in the budget. State accounts within the UTF are credited for this revenue. The U.S. Treasury reimburses states from the appropriate UTF state accounts for their benefit payments. These payments do not require an annual appropriation, but the reimbursements do count as federal budget outlays.

Generally, during economic expansions, FUTA and SUTA revenue collections will exceed UC outlays. During economic recessions, revenues generally will be less than UC outlays. For example, UTF outlays significantly exceeded trust fund revenue in FY2001-FY2004, and again starting in FY2008. From FY2005 to FY2007, UC revenue exceeded total UC outlays. Table 3 lists the total revenue and outlays associated with the UC program from FY200 1 through FY20 10 (estimated).

Outstanding Loans from the Federal Unemployment Account

If a state trust fund account becomes insolvent, a state may borrow federal funds.[9] DOL maintains a list of all states with loans and includes the loan amounts.[10] States are charged interest on loans that are not repaid by the end of the fiscal year in which they were obtained.

The American Recovery and Reinvestment Act of 2009 (P.L. 111-5, the 2009 stimulus package) temporarily waives interest payments, and no interest will accrue on interest payments that come due from the time the stimulus package was enacted (February 17, 2009) until December 31, 2010. Although states will not need to pay interest during this period, they must still repay the principal on the underlying loans according to the schedule provided in federal law. If a state does not pay back loaned funds within the prescribed amount of time or make good progress as determined by the U.S. Secretary of Labor, the state unemployment tax credit will be reduced.

FEDERAL ADDITIONAL COMPENSATION

P.L. 111-5 created the Federal Additional Compensation (FAC), a $25 weekly benefit supplement for individuals receiving benefits from all unemployment compensation programs: UC, EUC08, the Extended Benefit (EB) program, Disaster Unemployment Assistance (DUA), and Trade Adjustment Assistance (TAA). The authorization for the FAC $25 weekly benefit expired on May 29, 2010. It has not been extended by recent legislation (P.L. 111-205).

Table 3. Revenue and Spending Associated with Unemployment Compensation, FY2001 -FY2010 (in Billions of Dollars)

	2001	2002	2003	2004	2005	2006	2007	2008	2009	2010[a]
UC revenue, total	**27.8**	**27.5**	**33.2**	**39.3**	**41.8**	**43.0**	**41.2**	**39.4**	**37.8**	**51.3**
FUTA tax	6.9	6.6	6.5	6.6	6.7	7.1	7.3	7.2	6.7	6.8
State UC taxes	20.8	20.9	26.7	32.7	35.1	35.9	33.7	32.2	31.1	44.5
UC outlays, total	**31**	**53.8**	**57.4**	**40.9**	**35.0**	**34.3**	**34.7**	**41.7**	**117.2**	**155.1**
Regular benefits	27.3	42	42	36.9	31.2	30.2	31.4	38.1	75.3	84.1
Extended benefits	[b]	0.16	0.32	0.16	0.00	0.20	0.00	0.02	4.1	17.8
Emergency UC	—	7.9	11	4.1	—	—	—	3.6	32.7	43.6
Federal Additional Compensation	—	—	—	—	—	—	—	—	6.5	9.6
Administrative Costs	**3.6**	**3.7**	**4.1**	**3.9**	**3.8**	**3.9**	**3.7**	**3.9**	**4.3**	**5.9**

Source: U.S. Department of Labor, *UI Outlook*, January 2001-February 2010, and updates.

a. Estimated for 2010. Estimates assumed authorization for EUC08, EB, 100% federal EB financing, and FAC expired at the end of February.

b. Less than $5 million.

If an unemployed individual was receiving any type of unemployment benefit—UC, EUC08, EB, DUA, or TAA—prior to May 29, 2010 (May 30, 2010, for New York state), that individual will continue to receive the weekly FAC until he or she has exhausted all unemployment benefits from all unemployment programs (i.e., UC, EUC08, EB, DUA, and TAA) or until December 11, 2010 (December 12, 2010, for New York), whichever date comes first. Individuals who begin receiving unemployment benefits after May 29, 2010 (May 30, 2010, for New York state) will not receive the FAC.

EMERGENCY UNEMPLOYMENT COMPENSATION PROGRAM

On June 30, 2008, the President signed the Supplemental Appropriations Act of 2008 (P.L. 110- 252) into law. Title IV of this act created a new temporary unemployment insurance program, the EUC08 program. This is the eighth time Congress has created a federal temporary program that has extended unemployment compensation during an economic slowdown. Until February 16, 2009, the EUC08 program was financed with funds within the UTF. However, with the passage of P.L. 111-5, the EUC08 benefit is now 100% federally funded from general funds within the U.S. Treasury. State UC agencies administer the EUC08 benefit along with regular UC benefits.

On November 21, 2008, the President signed P.L. 110-449, the Unemployment Compensation Extension Act of 2008, into law. P.L. 110-449 expanded the potential duration of the EUC08 benefit from up to 13 weeks of EUC08 to a maximum of 20 weeks. It also created a second tier of benefits for workers in states with high unemployment of up to a maximum of an additional 13 weeks of tier II EUC08 benefits (for up to a cumulative 33 weeks of EUC08 benefits).

On February 27, 2009, the President signed the 2009 stimulus package, P.L. 111-5, known as the American Economic Recovery and Reinvestment Act, or ARRA. ARRA authorized the EUC08 program through December 2009. The 2009 stimulus package also contained temporary provisions for 100% federal financing of the EB program and to create an additional $25 weekly benefit for those receiving regular UC, EUC08, or EB. EUC08 benefits have been financed from the EUCA in the UTF. Starting from enactment of the 2009 stimulus package, however, EUC08 benefits are financed from general revenues through the termination of the EUC08 program.

On November 6, 2009, the President signed P.L. 111-92, the Worker, Homeownership, and Business Assistance Act of 2009, into law. P.L. 111-92 expanded benefits available in the EUC08 program. Tier I benefits continue to be up to 20 weeks in duration and tier II benefits are now 14 weeks in duration (compared with 13 previously) and no longer are dependent on a state's unemployment rate. The new tier III benefit provides up to 13 weeks of EUC08 benefits to those workers in states with an average unemployment rate of 6% or higher. The new tier IV benefit may provide up to an additional six weeks of benefits if the state unemployment rate is at least 8. 5%.[11]

On December 21, 2009, the President signed P.L. 111-118, the Department of Defense Appropriations Act of 2010, into law. P.L. 111-118 extended the EUC08 program, 100% federal financing of the EB program, and the $25 supplemental weekly benefit through February 28, 2010.

On March 2, 2010, the President signed P.L. 111-144, the Temporary Extension Act, which extended the EUC08 program, 100% federal financing of the EB program, and the $25 weekly supplemental benefit until April 5, 2010.

On April 15, 2010, the President signed P.L. 111-157, the Continuing Extension Act of 2010 into law. P.L. 111-157 extended the availability of EUC08, 100% federal financing of EB, and the $25 FAC benefit until the week ending on or before June 2, 2010.

On July 22, 2010, the President signed P.L. 111-205, the Unemployment Compensation Extension Act of 2010, into law. P.L. 111-205 extends the availability of EUC08 until the week ending on or before November 30, 2010.

See **Appendix B** for a summary of public laws, benefits, effective dates, and financing issues related to the EUC08 program.

Previous Temporary Unemployment Compensation Extensions

Previously, Congress acted seven times—in 1958, 1961, 1971, 1974, 1982, 1991, and 2002—to establish similar temporary programs of extended UC benefits. These programs extended the period an individual might claim UC benefits (ranging from an additional 6 to 33 weeks) and had expiration dates.[12] Some extensions took into account state economic conditions; many temporary programs considered the state's total TUR or the state's IUR or both.

EUC08 Benefit Amounts, Tiers, and Duration

The amount of the EUC08 benefit is the equivalent of the eligible individual's weekly regular UC benefit and includes any applicable dependents' allowances. The 2009 stimulus package, as amended, provides a federally financed, supplemental $25 per week benefit for unemployment compensation, including EUC08 tier I-tier IV benefits, for those individuals receiving unemployment benefits prior to May 29, 2010 (see section on "Federal Additional Compensation" above for more details on FAC expiration and "grandfathering").

Tier I

The maximum number of weeks an individual may be eligible for tier I EUC08 benefits is capped at 20 weeks. Some individuals may be eligible for fewer weeks of the tier I EUC08 benefits if their regular UC benefit entitlement was less than 26 weeks.

Tier II

Once an individual has exhausted tier I benefits, a second tier of EUC08 benefits may be available if the individual remains unemployed and satisfies the EUC08 conditions to entitlement. P.L. 111-92 expanded tier II benefits. They are now 14 weeks in duration (compared with 13 previously) and no longer are dependent on a state's unemployment rate.

Tier III

The new tier III benefit provides up to 13 weeks of EUC08 benefits to those workers in states with an average total unemployment rate of 6% or higher or in states with an average insured unemployment rate of 4% or higher.

Tier IV

The new tier IV benefit may provide up to an additional six weeks of benefits if the state average total unemployment rate is at least 8.5% or in states with an average insured unemployment rate of at least of 6%.

All Tiers Terminate November 30, 2010, with Grandfathering

All tiers of EUC08 benefits are temporary and expire on November 30, 2010. Those unemployed individuals who had qualified for a tier I, II, III, or

IV EUC08 benefit by November 27, 2010,[13] are "grandfathered" for their remaining weeks of eligibility for only that specific tier, and will continue to receive payments for the number of weeks they were deemed eligible. However, there will be no new entrants into any tier of the EUC08 program after the week that ends on November 30, 2010. In other words, to be eligible for an EUC08 tier I benefit, an individual must have exhausted his or her *regular* UC benefits before or during the week ending November 20, 2010,[14] so as to enter the first tier of EUC08 benefits during the week ending November 27, and be grandfathered for tier I benefits after November 30, 2010.

If an individual is eligible to continue to receive the tier I benefit after November 27, 2010, that individual would not be entitled to tier II benefits once those tier I benefits were exhausted. Similarly, if an individual is eligible to continue to receive the tier II benefit after November 27, 2010, that individual would not be entitled to tier III benefits once those tier II benefits were exhausted. Likewise, if an individual is eligible to continue to receive the tier III benefit after November 27, 2010, that individual would not be entitled to tier IV benefits once those tier III benefits were exhausted. No EUC08 benefits—regardless of tier—are payable for any week after April 30, 2011.

Tier I EUC08 Eligibility Requirements

First Claimed Regular UC Benefits On or After May 7, 2006

Applicants must have been eligible for regular UC benefits and have exhausted their rights to regular UC compensation with respect to a benefit year that expired during or after the week of May 6, 2007.[15] For most states, this would apply to individuals who had filed UC claims with an effective date of May 7, 2006, or later. For the state of New York this would apply to original claims filed with an effective date of May 1, 2006, or later.[16]

Exhausted Regular UC Benefit

The right to regular UC benefits for an individual must be exhausted to be eligible for EUC08 benefits. Although federal laws and regulations provide broad guidelines on regular UC benefit coverage and eligibility determination, the specifics of regular UC benefits are determined by each state. As noted earlier, this results in 53 different programs.[17] In particular, states determine

UC benefit eligibility, amount, and duration through state laws and program regulations.[18]

"20 Weeks" of Full-Time Insured Employment or Equivalent

In addition to all state requirements for regular UC eligibility, the EUC08 program requires claimants to have at least 20 weeks of full-time insured employment or the equivalent in insured wages in their base period. The definition of "20 weeks" is discussed in the "Methods for Determining 20 Weeks of Full-Time Insured Employment" section of this report.

Tier II EUC08 Eligibility Requirements

Exhausted Tier I EUC08 Benefit

The right to tier I EUC08 benefits must be exhausted to be eligible for the tier II EUC08 benefits.

Tier III EUC08 Eligibility Requirements

Exhausted Tier II EUC08 Benefit

The right to tier II EUC08 benefits must be exhausted to be eligible for the tier III EUC08 benefits. States have the ability to waive this requirement and pay tier III before tier II if doing so would aid in prompt payment of EUC08 benefits.

At or After the Period of Tier II EUC08 Exhaustion, the State Must Currently Have At Least 6% Unemployment Rate

The individual must have worked in a state with unemployment currently of at least 6% or an IUR of at least 4%. If the state's unemployment rate meets one of these conditions, a (still) unemployed tier II benefit exhaustee would be eligible for tier III benefits at that time.

Each Monday the Department of Labor issues its "Emergency Unemployment Compensation Trigger Notice" at *http://www.workforcesecurity.doleta.gov/unemploy/claims_arch.asp*. If the status column for tier III within the notice is "on" for a particular state's row, that state is considered to be high unemployment for the purposes of EUC08 tier III benefits.

No Retroactive Payments

No retroactive EUC08 payments exist for the period during which the individual had exhausted tier II benefits but the state did not meet the high unemployment criteria. However, once a state reaches the 6.0% level (and it has been at least 13 weeks since tier III benefits were previously available), a still unemployed tier II exhaustee would be able to receive tier III benefits.

Tier IV EUC08 Eligibility Requirements

Exhausted Tier I, Tier II, and Tier III EUC08 Benefits

The right to tier I, tier II, and tier III EUC08 benefits must be exhausted to be eligible for the tier IV EUC08 benefits.

At or After the Period of Tier III EUC08 Exhaustion, the State Must Currently Have At Least 8.5% Unemployment Rate

The individual must have worked in a state with unemployment currently of at least 8.5% or an IUR of at least 5%. If the state's unemployment rate meets one of these conditions, a (still) unemployed tier III benefit exhaustee would be eligible for tier IV benefits at that time.

Each Monday the Department of Labor issues its "Emergency Unemployment Compensation Trigger Notice" at *http://www.workforcesecurity.doleta.gov/unemploy/claims_arch.asp*. If the status column for tier IV benefits within the notice is "on" for a particular state's row, that state is considered to be high unemployment for the purposes of EUC08.

No Retroactive Payments

No retroactive EUC08 payments exist for the period during which the individual had exhausted tier IV benefits but the state did not meet the tier IV high unemployment criteria. However, once a state reaches the 8.5% level (and it has been at least 13 weeks since tier IV benefits were most recently available), a still unemployed tier III exhaustee would be able to receive benefits.

EUC08 Financing

Until February 16, 2009, the EUC08 program was federally financed from the extended unemployment compensation account (EUCA) within the Unemployment Trust Fund (UTF). With the passage of the 2009 stimulus package (P.L. 111-5), however, EUC08 is now financed from general funds of the U.S. Treasury through the expiration of the EUC08 program. States do not need to repay these funds.

EUC08 and EB Interactions

The EUC08 program should not be confused with the similarly named EB program (see description below). The EUC08 program is temporary and tiers I and II of EUC08 apply to all states while tier III and IV of EUC08 apply to states with high and very high unemployment, respectively. The EB program is permanently authorized and applies only to certain states on the basis of state unemployment conditions specified in law.

The EUC08 program allows states to determine which benefit, EB or EUC08, is paid first. Most states have opted to pay EUC08 benefits before EB. Alaska has opted to pay EB before EUC08 benefits.

An exception to the payment order may be made if an individual claimed EB for at least one week of unemployment after exhausting the first two tiers of EUC08 and prior to the enactment P.L. 111-92, which created new EUC08 tiers III and IV. P.L. 111-92 gives states the option of paying EB to an otherwise eligible individual prior to the payment of any EUC08 benefits that are payable on account of the Worker Assistance Act amendments to the EUC08 program (or vice versa in the case of Alaska).

EXTENDED BENEFIT PROGRAM

The EB program was established by the Federal-State Extended Unemployment Compensation Act of 1970 (EUCA), P.L. 9 1-373 (26 U.S.C. 3304, note). EUCA may extend receipt of unemployment benefits (extended benefits) at the state level if certain economic situations exist within the state.

The EB program is triggered when a state's IUR[19] or TUR[20] reaches certain levels. All states must pay up to 13 weeks of EB if the IUR for the previous 13 weeks is at least 5% and is 120% of the average of the rates for the same 13-week period in each of the two previous years. There are two other optional thresholds that states may choose. (States may choose one, two, or none.) If the state has chosen a given option, they would provide the following:

- Option 1: an additional 13 weeks of benefits if the state's IUR is at least 6%, regardless of previous years' averages.
- Option 2: an additional 13 weeks of benefits if the state's TUR is at least 6.5% and is at least 110% of the state's average TUR for the same 13 weeks in either of the previous two years; an additional 20 weeks of benefits if the TUR is at least 8% and is at least 110% of the state's average TUR for the same 13 weeks in either of the previous two years.

Each state's IUR and TUR are determined by the state of residence (agent state) of the unemployed worker rather than by the state of employment (liable state). EB benefits are not "grandfathered" when a state triggers "off" the program; that is, EB benefit payments in the state cease immediately.

EB Triggers May be Reviewed in 2010

The President's 2010 budget outline suggested the EB program be modified to make the UC system more responsive to changing economic conditions. The current EB triggers have been criticized for deploying in many states long after a recession has started, for not deploying at all in some states with high unemployment, and for triggering off too quickly in some states. Analysts cite several reasons for this: (1) the general long-term decline in unemployment rates has made the current triggers irrelevant; (2) the rate and lookback provisions work against each other; and (3) amendments to the program in the early 1980s changed the IUR calculation in a way that made EB activation less likely.[21]

At the same time, analysts and legislators have also questioned the use of emergency extended programs (such as EUC08) because these temporary programs can be subject to delays related to the recognition of a recession and legislative activity. As a result, there is interest in modifying the EB program, and especially the EB triggers, so that the EB program can deliver timely and well- targeted benefits.

Some of the issues concerning the EB trigger include national- versus state-level triggers, use of the IUR versus the TUR, and the use of lookbacks that compare current unemployment with conditions one and two years earlier.

The EB trigger is composed of two components, a *level* and a *lookback.* The EB is said to be triggered "on" in a state when both components have met or exceeded the thresholds. The *level* component of a trigger is a threshold rate, such as the IUR or the TUR. The *lookback* component compares the current period's level (rate) to the level in the same period in some reference time such as the previous two years.

A national trigger may seem appropriate because the definition of a recession is that it is national in scope, and the federal government's interest in reversing an economic decline is national as well. On the other hand, recessions have variations in its regional impact. A national trigger could cause extended benefits to be paid to individuals in states that do not face unusually weak labor markets. Regional or sub-regional triggers have also been suggested as a means to improve the targeting of benefits, because labor markets can span state boundaries or be confined to rural or urban areas within a state (especially where a single industry is involved). It would be very difficult, however, to define appropriate regional or sub-state boundaries. There is also concern about data accuracy and availability at regional or sub-state levels. With the EUC08 program, Congress opted for a combination of national- and state-level triggers: EUC08 tiers I and II provide benefits to all unemployed workers, and EUC08 tiers III and IV provide additional weeks of benefits to unemployed workers in states that face high unemployment.

The IUR and the TUR have been used as triggers for the EB and EUC08 programs, and each has merits as well as drawbacks. The calculation of the IUR is the ratio of the number of people claiming regular UC benefits to the number of insured workers. The IUR is arguably the more accurate indication of actual demand for EB. The IUR's numerator can change with noneconomic factors such as state eligibility rules and administrative practices, however, and this in turn can affect whether the EB is activated in a particular state. The TUR is defined as the number of all unemployed individuals divided by the size of the civilian labor force (employed and unemployed). The TUR represents a larger population because it includes uninsured workers (such as the self-employed) and because it includes all unemployed workers, including those who failed to qualify for regular UC benefits or who have exhausted regular UC. Recent studies have suggested that whether an IUR or TUR trigger is used, the secular decline in unemployment over the past several decades has resulted in the current trigger levels being relatively difficult to attain.

Lookbacks (e.g., the base EB requirement that the IUR requirement be at least 120% of the average of the rates for the same 13-week period in the each of the previous two years) are useful for measuring changes in unemployment relative to a baseline, but have also been controversial. The EB lookback has been criticized for forcing the trigger off too quickly, before the end of a recession. This can occur, for example, when high unemployment rates reach a—still high— plateau and the rate change from the reference period falls below 20% (in the case of a lookback requirement of 120%). Some have proposed that the trigger not include a lookback; others have suggested that the trigger refer to a fixed point in time at some date before the declaration of a recession.

The Advisory Council on Unemployment Compensation recommended in 1994 that the EB program use a state TUR of 6.5%, and that the EB program not use a lookback.

Other potential EB triggers could include the increase in the number of unemployed over a period such as the previous year; the increase in the number of long-term unemployed (unemployed for over 26 weeks); or changes in the number of UC exhaustees. Although the UC exhaustion rate is intuitively appealing, a potential problem with this trigger includes a built-in delay of up to 26 weeks until benefit exhaustion that could prevent timely launch of the EB program.

It would be important in any reform to build in a mechanism for reviewing and updating EB triggers.

EB Eligibility Requirements Beyond Requirements for Regular UC

The EB program imposes additional federal restrictions on individual eligibility for benefits beyond the state requirements for regular UC. The EB program requires that a worker make a “systematic and sustained” work search. Furthermore, the worker may not receive benefits if he or she refused an offer of “suitable” work, which is defined as “any work within such individual’s capabilities”. In addition, P.L. 97-3 5, among other items, amended the EUCA to require that claimants work at least 20 weeks of full-time insured employment or equivalent in insured wages during their base period.

The 2009 stimulus package affects a further requirement for EB eligibility. As the EB program has operated in the past, a beneficiary had to be *within* their original "benefit year"[22] when the EB program triggered "on" in their state in order to receive EB benefits. Thus, on the condition that the state triggered "on" during an individual's benefit year, he or she could receive EB benefits during the benefit year, or even after the benefit year expired, that is, at the time he or she exhausted regular unemployment compensation or EUC08 benefits even if this occurred after the expiration of the benefit year. However, if the state's most recent EB period triggered on *after* the individual's benefit year ended, the beneficiary would not receive EB. As a result, in states that have recently triggered "on" to EB because of rising unemployment rates, many individuals may be ineligible for EB benefits. For example, if an individual's benefit year expired in July 2008, this person would be ineligible for EB benefits if his or her state triggered "on" for EB in November 2008.

Under the 2009 stimulus package (as amended), states have the option of ignoring the benefit year requirement and instead using EUC08 exhaustion as an eligibility requirement, as long as the state's EB period falls between enactment of the stimulus package and November 30, 2010. This has the effect of allowing more individuals to be eligible for the EB program.[23]

As described above, the EUC08 program contains a "reachback" clause under which EUC08 benefits were made available to individuals who had exhausted regular UC benefits with respect to a benefit year that expired during or after the week of May 6, 2007. Before the stimulus package, many individuals who had exhausted EUC08 benefits would have been ineligible for EB benefits if the state triggered "on" for EB after their benefit year expired. Under the stimulus package, however, all individuals who have exhausted EUC08 benefits would be eligible for EB benefits, regardless of the timing of their benefit years.

Methods for Determining 20 Weeks of Full-Time Insured Employment

States use one, two, or three different methods for determining an "equivalent" to 20 weeks of full-time insured employment. These methods are described in both law (Section 202(a)(5) of the EUCA) and regulation (20 CFR 615.4(b)). In practice, states that require any of these three methods for receipt of regular UC benefits *and* do not allow for exceptions to those requirements do not need to establish that the worker meets the 20 weeks full-time insured employment. The three methods are listed below:

- earnings in the base period equal to at least 1.5 times the high-quarter wages; or
- earnings in the base period of at least 40 times the most recent weekly benefit amount, and if this alternative is adopted, it shall use the weekly benefit amount (including dependents' allowances) payable for a week of total unemployment (before any reduction because of earnings, pensions or other requirements) that applied to the most recent week of regular benefits; or
- earnings in the base period equal to at least 20 weeks of full-time insured employment, and if this alternative is adopted, the term "full-time" shall have the meaning provided by the state law.

The base period may be the regular base period or, if applicable in the state, the period may be the alternative base period or the extended base period if that determined the regular UC benefit.

The underlying reasoning behind the requirements seems to be the following:

- Because there are 13 weeks in a quarter, 1.5 times the high-quarter wage is roughly equivalent to 1.5 times 13 weeks of wages or about 20 weeks of wages. (Many states require high quarterly earnings of under $2,000, which works out to less than $4/hour under full-time assumptions. This is less than the federal minimum wage of $5.85/hour.)
- Similarly, because the weekly benefit amount is roughly equivalent to half the average weekly wage, 40 times the weekly benefit amount is roughly equivalent to 20 weeks of wages.

2009 Stimulus Provisions Affecting EB Level and Duration

The EB program provides for additional weeks of UC benefits. As described earlier, all states must pay up to a maximum of 13 weeks during periods of high unemployment, and certain states that have chosen additional, optional triggers may pay up to a maximum of 20 weeks during periods of extremely high unemployment. The 2009 stimulus package (as amended) provided a supplemental $25 weekly benefit for those individuals receiving unemployment benefits prior to May 29, 2010, including EB (see section on

"Federal Additional Compensation" above for more details on FAC expiration and "grandfathering").

EB benefits on interstate claims are limited to two extra weeks unless both the agent state (e.g., Texas) and liable state (e.g., Louisiana) are both in an EB period.

2009 Stimulus Provisions Affecting EB Financing

Under permanent law, EB benefits are funded half (50%) by the federal government through its account for that purpose in the UTF. States fund the other half (50%) through their state accounts in the UTF. The federal government pays 100% of EB *administrative* costs.

The 2009 stimulus package, as amended, temporarily changes the federal-state funding arrangement. The federal government finances 100% of EB benefits through November 30, 2010, through the EUCA of the UTF, with the exception of "non-sharable" benefits (generally, these are former state and local employees' EB benefits). The EB program's 100% federal financing has prompted some states to adopt the optional triggers to provide 20 weeks of extended benefits. The exception for non-sharable benefits, however, has made some states reluctant to adopt the optional 20-week EB triggers, or the stimulus provision that allows them to use EUC08 exhaustion rather than benefit year as a requirement for EB eligibility.

For individuals who were receiving EB payments on November 30, 2010, the federal government will continue to pay 100% of EB benefits for the duration of these individuals' benefits (but not for new entrants to the EB program starting after that date). The stimulus package also continues the temporary suspension of the waiting week requirement for federal funding until the week ending on or before May 30, 2011.[24]

SHORT-TIME COMPENSATION (WORK SHARING)

Short-time compensation (STC) is a program within the federal-state unemployment compensation system. Seventeen states operate STC programs.

STC is a regular unemployment benefit, pro-rated for a partial work reduction, that is offered within the context of a temporary work sharing arrangement. Under a work sharing arrangement, a firm that is faced with a need to downsize temporarily reduces work hours for many or all workers instead of laying off a smaller number of workers. For example, an employer might reduce the work hours of the entire workforce by 20%, from five to four days a week, in lieu of laying off 20% of the workforce.

States with STC programs require employers who seek STC for their workers to submit a formal work sharing plan for approval. Once the state has approved an employer's plan, the work- sharing employees receive pro-rated unemployment compensation, or STC. In the above example, the amount of STC provided to each worker would be 20% of the unemployment benefit that a worker would have received had he or she been laid off.

Employers have used STC combined with work sharing arrangements to reduce labor costs while retaining highly skilled workers. Work sharing can also reduce employers' recruitment and training costs by making it unnecessary to recruit new employees when business improves. On the employee's side, work sharing arrangements combined with STC can spread more moderate earnings reductions across more employees—as opposed to imposing significant hardship on a few. Work sharing and STC cannot, however, avert layoffs or plant closings if a company's financial situation is dire. In addition, some employers may choose not to adopt work sharing because laying off workers may be a less expensive alternative.

STC benefits are charged to employers according to the experience rating rules of a state's regular unemployment program. Therefore, a firm generally incurs no more in UI tax costs by using STC than it would through layoffs. Seven states also impose additional tax provisions on work sharing employers, in order to ensure that employers who already pay the maximum state unemployment tax rate share in the burden.

Currently, only 18 states operate STC programs to support work sharing arrangements. Through the end of 2008, the STC program has never constituted more than about 1% of unemployment benefits paid annually across the United States, although very preliminary data for the first three quarters of 2009 indicate that this ratio may recently have risen to as high as 2%. The reasons for low state and employer take-up of the STC program are not completely clear, but a key cause would appear to be ambiguity in the 1992 federal law that authorizes STC. Because of this ambiguity, the U.S. Department of Labor (DOL) has not provided guidance or technical assistance on STC to the states since 1992. A more active public policy would require either DOL reinterpretation of the 1992 law or congressional action to either clarify federal law or give the Secretary of Labor authority to determine needed additional provisions.[25]

POLICY PROPOSALS THAT TARGET UNEMPLOYMENT BENEFIT EXHAUSTEES

Recent congressional hearings have raised the issue of how to aid long-term unemployed workers, especially those individuals who have exhausted all available unemployment benefits.[26] As of June 2010, about 46% of unemployed individuals had been without a job for more than 26 weeks.[27] These long-term unemployed workers are at risk of exhausting current benefits while remaining unemployed.[28] A number of ideas have been advanced to provide additional income or employment support to these individuals. Five popular policy strategies include the following:

- **Work sharing:** Described in more detail above, the Short-Time Compensation (STC) program—also known as "work sharing"—provides pro-rated unemployment benefits to workers whose hours have been reduced in lieu of a layoff, thereby retaining workers and avoiding unemployment.[29] Although STC does not address unemployment benefit exhaustees directly, it attempts to mitigate unemployment by preventing additional layoffs. Currently, 18 states have STC programs. But several pieces of proposed legislation seek to provide support for states to enact or expand STC programs.[30]
- **Subsidized jobs:** One way to deliver support for unemployment benefit exhaustees is by creating jobs.[31] As proposed, H.R. 4812, the Local Jobs for America Act, would provide federal funding to save and create local jobs. Additionally, an earlier version of P.L. 111-205 proposed aid for subsidized employment through the TANF Emergency Contingency Fund (see below).
- **Self-Employment Assistance (SEA):** The SEA program provides a weekly allowance, which is similar to a regular UC benefit in amount and duration, to individuals who are otherwise eligible for unemployment benefits and are participating full-time in self-employment activities. SEA waives state job search requirements so that unemployed workers can start their own business while receiving income support. SEA is available only to UC beneficiaries who have been identified as likely to exhaust their benefits.[32] Currently, only eight states have active SEA programs. Although there are no current legislative proposals related to SEA a recent Senate Committee on

Finance hearing highlighted the program as a potential source of aid to keep workers from becoming exhaustees.[33]

- **Tier V (of EUC08):** Some recent policy discussion has focused on the appropriate length of unemployment benefits; in particular, whether the creation of a tier V of the EUC08 program—or other additional weeks of unemployment benefits—is warranted.[34] On August 4, 2010, Senator Stabenow introduced S. 3706, which proposes an additional tier of EUC08 benefits consisting of 20 weeks for eligible individuals who have worked in states with an average total unemployment rate of at least 7.5%.
- **TANF Emergency Contingency Fund (ECF):** The 2009 stimulus package (ARRA, P.L. 111-5) created an Emergency Contingency Fund (ECF) within the Temporary Assistance for Needy Families (TANF) block grant to states, Indian tribes, and the territories. States, Indian tribes, and the territories are reimbursed 80% of the costs of increased expenditures on direct aid to families that fall into three categories: (1) basic assistance, which resembles traditional cash welfare; (2) non-recurrent short-term (e.g., emergency) aid; and (3) subsidized employment.[35] Currently, the ECF is temporarily funded for two years, FY2009 and FY2010. An earlier version of P.L. 111-205 would have extended the fund through FY20 11. H.R. 5893 also proposes to extend the ECF—and to rename it the "Emergency Fund for Job Creation and Assistance"—through FY20 11.

Legislative Issues

111th Congress

2010 Budget

The President's 2010 budget highlighted the need for legislation to make the UC system more responsive to changing economic conditions, both as an automatic stabilizer and as an effective social safety net. In a letter transmitting the Views and Estimates of the House Committee on Ways and Means concerning 2010 budget issues within its purview, the committee states that it will continue to monitor the effectiveness of the 2009 stimulus package (ARRA), including unemployment provisions in the package.

An ongoing question concerns whether the EB program can be altered so that it makes benefits available more quickly to long-term unemployed workers, thereby avoiding the delays associated with legislation to create special, temporary extended unemployment programs. Although specifics are not yet available, reforms may center around the EB program and its trigger mechanism. Potential issues may include the appropriateness of national versus state or regional triggers, the use of the IUR versus the TUR, the trigger level, and the use of "lookbacks" to unemployment in a reference period. (These issues are discussed in more detail in the "Extended Benefit Program" section of this report.)

P.L. 111-5, The American Recovery and Reinvestment Act of 2009

ARRA (P.L. 111-5, the 2009 stimulus package) contained a number of important provisions that affect unemployment benefits. These provisions included extension of the EUC08 program through December 2009; temporary 100% federal financing of the EB program; up to $7 billion for modernization of state unemployment programs; a temporary $25 per week supplemental benefit for regular UC, EB, EUC08, TAA and DUA benefits; temporary tax relief for unemployment benefits; and a temporary suspension of interest accrual on loans to insolvent state UTF funds.[36]

Unemployment Compensation Modernization

The 2009 stimulus package provided for a special transfer of up to $7 billion in federal monies to state unemployment programs as "incentive payments" for changing certain state UC laws. The funds are transferred from the federal unemployment account (FUA) in the UTF to qualifying states' UTF accounts. The maximum incentive payment allowable for a state is calculated using the methods used in Reed Act distributions.

For a state to receive one-third of its potential distribution it must enact an alternative base period, which ensures the last completed quarter of a worker's employment is counted when determining eligibility for unemployment benefits. The remaining two-thirds of the $7 billion are distributed to states contingent on their qualifying for the first one-third, plus state law containing at least two of the following four provisions: (1) permit former part-time workers to seek part-time work; (2) permit voluntary separations from employment for compelling family reasons; (3) provide extended compensation to UC recipients in training programs for high-demand occupations; or (4) provide dependents allowances to UC recipients with dependents.

In addition to the $7 billion in conditional transfers, the package immediately transferred a total of $500 million to the states for the administration of UC programs, without conditions. These funds could be used to pay for (1) administration of the new provisions, if any, enacted in order to receive shares of the $7 billion in special incentive payments; (2) improvement of outreach to individuals who might be eligible for regular unemployment compensation by virtue of the expansion provisions; (3) improvement of unemployment benefit and tax operations, including responding to increased demand for unemployment compensation; and (4) staff-assisted reemployment services for unemployment compensation claimants.

Federal Additional Compensation

The 2009 stimulus package, as amended, temporarily increased benefits by $25 per week. This supplemental FAC benefit expired on May 29, 2010. Prior to May 29, 2010, it was available to all individuals receiving regular UC, EB, EUC08, DUA, and TAA benefits. This supplemental benefit is grandfathered for individuals who had been receiving the FAC and have not exhausted the right to all unemployment benefits as of May 29, 2010; however, no federal additional compensation is payable after December 11, 2010. The supplemental benefit is financed by the federal government from general revenues and does not need to be repaid.

ARRA Provisions Affecting the EUC08 Program

The 2009 stimulus package, as amended, also extended the temporary EUC08 program through May 29, 2010 (May 30, 2010, for New York state). Following enactment of the stimulus package, the extension of EUC08 benefits began to be paid from the general funds of the U.S. Treasury and does not need to be repaid.

Temporary Waiver of Interest Payments and the Accrual of Interest on Advances to State Unemployment Funds

The stimulus package provides temporary relief to states that borrow from the Federal Unemployment Account of the Unemployment Trust Fund. The interest payments due between enactment of the stimulus package (February 17, 2009) through December 31, 2010, would be deemed to have been made by the state. In addition, no interest on advances accrue during the period.

Temporary 100% EB Financing and Changes to EB Eligibility

The 2009 stimulus package (as amended) temporarily changes the federal-state funding arrangement for the EB program. The federal government will finance 100% of EB benefits through November 30, 2010, with the exception of "non-sharable" (state and local government employees') EB benefits, as those benefits are also not subject to the permanent law 50% federal financing provisions. The 100% federal financing of EB benefits takes place through the EUCA in the UTF. After the 100% federal financing authorization ends, EB financing would revert to 50% state financing and 50% federal financing, although 100% financing would be grandfathered for individuals who were receiving EB during the week that the authorization of 100% federal financing was terminated. Consistent with this change in financing requirements, the stimulus package also continues the temporary suspension of the waiting week requirement for federal funding until the week ending before May 30, 2011. Under the waiting week requirement, now temporarily suspended, states that do not require a one-week UC waiting period, or have an exception for any reason to the waiting period, paid 100% of the first week of EB.

The 2009 stimulus package also temporarily allows states the option of expanding EB eligibility, by ignoring the benefit year requirement and instead using EUC08 exhaustion as an eligibility requirement for EB (as long as the state is triggered "on" for EB) until the expiration of the EUC08 program. As the EB program has operated in the past, a beneficiary had to be within his or her original "benefit year" when the EB program triggered "on" in the state in order to receive EB benefits. Even though a number of states triggered "on" for EB in the second half of 2008, the benefit year requirement cause numerous individuals to be ineligible for EB because their benefit years had expired before the state triggered "on." Allowing states to use EUC08 exhaustion as an eligibility requirement instead will cause more individuals to be eligible for the EB program. Temporary Suspension of Federal Income Tax on Unemployment Benefits.

ARRA (P.L. 111-5) provided tax relief to the unemployed through the exemption of the first $2,400 of benefits from income taxation in tax year 2009. S. 155 and H.R. 155 proposed all unemployment benefits be exempt.

P.L. 111-92, The Worker, Homeownership and Business Assistance Act of 2009

The President signed P.L. 111-92, the Worker, Homeownership and Business Assistance Act of 2009, into law on November 6, 2009. The law created an additional (new second) tier of up to 14 weeks of benefits, without regard to state unemployment rates. The law also created a fourth tier of up to an additional six weeks of EUC08 benefits in states with unemployment rates of at least 8.5%. Other measures included in the proposal concerned eligibility for food stamp payments (benefit eligibility and determination would not consider the $25 additional federal unemployment benefit established in ARRA legislation); railroad workers (who have their own unemployment insurance system) would receive approximately the same increase in potential benefits; and the authorization of the 0.2% FUTA surtax is extended through 2010 and the first six months of calendar year 2011.

P.L. 111-118, The Department of Defense Appropriations Act

On December 19, 2009, the President signed P.L. 111-118, the Department of Defense Appropriations Act of 2010, into law. P.L. 111-118 extended the EUC08 program through the end of February 2010. The law also extended the 100% federal financing of the EB program and the $25 supplemental weekly benefit through end-February 2010.

P.L. 111-144, The Temporary Extension Act of 2010

On March 2, 2010, the President signed P.L. 111-144, the Temporary Extension Act of 2010. P.L. 111-144 extended three temporary provisions through April 5, 2010: EUC08, the $25 supplemental weekly benefit, and 100% federal EB financing. The Senate passed H.R. 4691 without amendment on March 2, 2010, and the President signed the bill that day.

P.L. 111-157, The Continuing Extension Act of 2010

On April 15, 2010, the President signed P.L. 111-157, the Continuing Extension Act of 2010 into law. P.L. 111-157 extends the availability of EUC08, 100% federal financing of EB, and the $25 FAC benefit, until the week ending on or before June 2, 2010.

P.L. 111-205, The Unemployment Compensation Extension Act of 2010

On July 22, 2010, the President signed P.L. 111-205, the Unemployment Compensation Extension Act of 2010, into law. P.L. 111-205 extends the availability of EUC08 and 100% federal financing of EB through November 30, 2010. It does not extend the $25 FAC benefit, which expired May 29, 2010.

Current Legislation

S. 3706, the Americans Want to Work Act, was introduced on August 4, 2010. S. 3706 would create an additional tier of EUC08 benefits. As proposed by S. 3706, this new tier of EUC08 would provide up to 20 weeks of additional unemployment benefits to eligible individuals who worked in states with an average total unemployment rate of at least 7.5%.

The House passed H.R. 5618, the Restoration of Emergency Unemployment Compensation Act of 2010, on July 1, 2010. H.R. 5618 would extend the availability of EUC08 and 100% federal financing of EB through the end of November 2010. There is, however, no extension of the weekly $25 FAC benefit in this bill. H.R. 5618 does contain a provision that requires states not to reduce weekly unemployment benefits in order to be eligible for EUC08 funds. No spending offsets are included in H.R. 5618.

S. 3520, the Unemployment Insurance Extension Act of 2010, was introduced on June 22, 2010. S. 3520 would extend EUC08, 100% federal financing of EB, and the weekly $25 FAC benefit through December 2010. It does not contain any spending offsets or provisions related to restrictions on unemployment benefit reductions by states.

On June 30, 2010, H.R. 5647, the Responsible COBRA, Unemployment, and Poverty Extension Act, was introduced. H.R. 5647 would extend the availability of EUC08 and 100% federal financing of EB through the end of September 2010. It would not extend the weekly $25 FAC benefit or require states not to reduce weekly unemployment benefits in order to receive EUC08 funds. In addition, H.R. 5647 includes a provision that fully offsets spending proposed in the bill with unobligated balances from P.L. 111-5, the American Recovery and Reinvestment Act of 2009.

S. 3551, the Fiscally Responsible Relief for Our States Act of 2010, also introduced on June 30, 2010, would extend the availability of EUC08 and 100% federal financing of EB through the end of November 2010. This bill does not contain an extension of FAC or a requirement that states not reduce weekly unemployment benefits in order to be eligible for EUC08 funds. S. 3551 does propose spending offsets, including the use of unobligated balances from P.L. 111-5.

H.R. 4183 would extend the authorization of the EUC08 program through March 2011. It also would extend the FAC benefit as well as the 100% federal financing for EB through March 2011. Additionally, it would provide 100% federal financing for short-time compensation benefits through March 2011.[37]

S. 2831 would extend the authorization of the EUC08 program through December 2010. It would also extend the FAC benefit as well as the 100%

federal financing for EB through December 2010. The bill would allow the unemployed to opt to continue to receive their remaining EUC08 entitlements rather than reapply for UC at the end of their benefit year. It would suspend the federal taxation of the first $2400 of unemployment benefits through 2010. The bill would also require the U.S. Department of Labor to conduct a study on the implementation of the EUC08 program. Additionally, S. 2831 provides 100% federal financing for short-time compensation benefits through 2011.

S. 1646, the Keep Americans Working Act, would provide federal financing to states for 100% of benefits paid to workers who participate in an STC program, contingent on employer certification that health and retirement benefits are not affected by participation in the STC program. The bill would also provide start-up grants to states and would allow the DOL to reimburse states for administrative expenses. Representative DeLauro has introduced a companion bill, H.R. 4135, in the House of Representatives. Senator Reed included substantially the same STC provisions from S. 1646 in S. 2831, the Helping Unemployed Workers Act. Representative McDermott introduced H.R. 4183, the Helping Unemployment Workers Act, which would require the Secretary of Labor to pay 100% of STC benefits to the unemployment trust fund accounts of states whose STC programs have been certified by the Secretary of Labor.

APPENDIX A. UNEMPLOYMENT INSURANCE BENEFITS

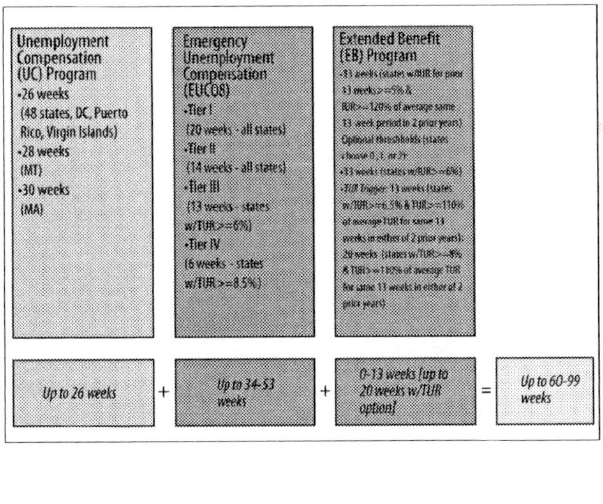

Source: CRS.

Figure A-1. Unemployment Insurance: Available Unemployment Benefits

Appendix B. Summary of EUC08 Program

Table B-1. Emergency Unemployment Compensation Program: Public Law, Benefits, Effective Dates, and Financing

Public Law	Benefit Tiers and Availability	Dates in Effect and Financing
Supplemental Appropriations Act of 2008, Title IV Emergency Unemployment Compensation (P.L. 110-252), signed June 30, 2008	13 weeks (all states)	7/6/2008-3/29/2009 (No benefits past 7/4/2009) Funded by federal EUCA funds within UTF.
Unemployment Compensation Extension Act of 2008 (P.L. 110-449), signed November 21, 2008.	Tier I: 20 weeks (all states) Tier II: 13 additional weeks (33 weeks total) if state TUR is 6% or higher or IUR is 4% or higher	11/23/2008-3/29/2009 (No benefits past 8/29/2009) Funded by federal EUCA funds within UTF.
American Recovery and Reinvestment Act of 2009 (P.L. 111-5), signed February 17, 2009.	Same as above.	2/22/2009-2/26/2009 (No benefits past 6/6/2010)
	[Note this included several other interventions that augmented UC benefits. The Federal Additional Compensation (FAC) benefit of $25/ week for those receiving UC, EUC08, EB, DUA, or TAA. At state option, EB benefit year could be calculated based upon exhausting EUC08 benefits. 100% federal financing of EB program. First $2400 of unemployment benefits were excluded from income tax in 2009.]	Funded by general fund of the Treasury. (Additionally, the FAC program is funded by the general fund of the Treasury. The 100% financing of the EB program is funded by the EUCA funds within the UTF.)
Worker, Homeowner, and Business Assistance Act of 2009 (P.L. 111-92), signed November 6, 2009.	Tier I: 20 weeks (all states) Tier II: 14 additional weeks (34 weeks total, all states) Tier III: 13 additional weeks if state TUR is 6% or higher	11/8/2009-12/26/2009 (No benefits past 6/6/2010) Funded by general fund of the Treasury.

Table B- 1. (Continued)

Public Law	Benefit Tiers and Availability	Dates in Effect and Financing
	or IUR is 4% or higher (47 weeks total) Tier IV: 6 additional weeks if state TUR is 8.5% or higher or IUR is 6% or higher (53 weeks total) [Note this included a 1.5 year extension of the Federal Unemployment Tax Act (FUTA) surtax.]	Extended FUTA surtax through June 2011. Estimated revenues collected from FUTA surtax provision were $2.578 billion and offset the estimated direct spending costs for unemployment insurance provisions of $2.42 billion.
Department of Defense Appropria-tions Act, 2010 (P.L. 111-118), signed December 19, 2009.	Same as above.	12/27/2009-2/27/2010 (No benefits past 7/31/2010) Funded by general fund of the Treasury.
Temporary Extension Act of 2010 (P.L. 111-144), signed March 2, 2010.	Same as above.	2/28/2010-4/3/2010 (No benefits past 9/4/2010) Funded by general fund of the Treasury.
The Continuing Extension Act of 2010 (P.L. 111-157), signed April 15, 2010	Same as above.	4/3/2010-6/2/2010 (No benefits past 11/6/ 2010) Funded by general fund of the Treasury.
The Unemployment Compensation Extension Act of 2010,. (P.L. 111-205), signed July 22, 2010.	Same as above. [Note this did not include an extension of the Federal Additional Compensation (FAC) benefit of $25/week for those receiving UC, EUC08, EB, DUA, or TAA. The FAC expired on May 29, 2010.]	6/2/2010-11/30/2010 (No benefits past 4/30/ 2011) Funded by general fund of the Treasury.

Source: CRS.

End Notes

[1] Montana provides 28 weeks and Massachusetts provides 30 weeks of regular unemployment benefits.

[2] The other temporary programs became effective in 1958, 1961, 1972, 1975, 1982, 1991, and 2002. For details on these programs, see CRS Report RL34340, *Extending Unemployment Compensation Benefits During Recessions*, by Julie M. Whittaker.

[3] See, for example, President Franklin Roosevelt's remarks at the signing of the Social Security Act at http://www.ssa.gov/history/fdrstmts.html#signing.

[4] For more information on unemployment modernization provisions in the American Recovery and Reinvestment Act of 2009 (P.L. 111-5), please see CRS Report R40368, *Unemployment Insurance Provisions in the American Recovery and Reinvestment Act of 2009*, by Alison M. Shelton and Julie M. Whittaker.

[5] In the *2010 Comparison of State Unemployment Insurance Laws* the following states used the measure of "weeks" in determination of eligibility or benefit amount: New Jersey, Ohio, and Pennsylvania. Only Washington appears to use the number of hours worked in eligibility or benefit determination.

[6] The temporary, federally financed EUC08 program offers up to 53 additional weeks of unemployment benefits for workers in states with certain economic conditions. The permanent federal-state EB program offers benefits for an additional 13 to 20 weeks in states with unemployment rates above certain levels. The EB and EUC08 programs are discussed later in this report.

[7] For a more detailed description of UC financing, see CRS Report RS22077, *Unemployment Compensation (UC) and the Unemployment Trust Fund (UTF): Funding UC Benefits*, by Julie M. Whittaker.

[8] Employers who are required to provide unemployment insurance coverage, but who are not required to pay the FUTA tax, generally reimburse state governments for the benefit payments related to their workers. States are reimbursed for expenditures related to federal workers by the federal government.

[9] For detailed information on loans to the states within the UTF, see CRS Report RS22954, *The Unemployment Trust Fund (UTF): State Insolvency and Federal Loans to States*, by Julie M. Whittaker.

[10] See http://www.workforcesecurity.doleta.gov/unemploy/budget.asp#tfloans.

[11] For details on the EUC08 program, see CRS Report RS22915, *Temporary Extension of Unemployment Benefits: Emergency Unemployment Compensation (EUC08)*, by Katelin P. Isaacs, Julie M. Whittaker, and Alison M. Shelton.

[12] For more information on these programs, see CRS Report RL34340, *Extending Unemployment Compensation Benefits During Recessions*, by Julie M. Whittaker.

[13] May 28, 2010, for New York state.

[14] May 21, 2010, for New York state.

[15] Arkansas has a unique approach to calculating a benefit year. In Arkansas, the benefit year begins the first day of the quarter in which an individual files a valid UC claim. Thus, it is unlikely that many individuals in Arkansas who filed UC claims before July 2006 would be eligible to receive EUC08 benefits.

[16] Note that the effective date is not necessarily the actual date when an individual filed for UC. A claim filed on May 10, 2006, may have had an earlier effective date if a state allows retroactive claims.

[17] The 50 states, the District of Columbia, Puerto Rico, and the Virgin Islands provide UC benefits to their workers.

[18] Individuals in the Massachusetts and Montana UC programs may have regular UC durations that exceed 26 weeks. Those additional weeks are not used to calculate EUC08 duration.

[19] The IUR is the ratio of UC claimants divided by individuals in UC-covered jobs. The IUR is substantially different than the TUR because it excludes several important groups: self-employed workers, unpaid family workers, workers in certain not-for-profit organizations, and several other, primarily seasonal, categories of workers. In addition to those unemployed workers whose last jobs were in the excluded employment, the insured unemployed rate excludes the following: those who have exhausted their UC benefits (even if they receive EB or EUC08 benefits); new entrants or reentrants to the labor force; disqualified workers whose unemployment is considered to have resulted from their own actions rather than from economic conditions; and, eligible unemployed persons who do not file for benefits.

[20] The TUR is the ratio of unemployed workers to all workers (employed and unemployed) in the labor market. The TUR is essentially a weekly version of the unemployment rate published by the Bureau of Labor Statistics and based on data from the BLS' monthly Current Population Survey.

[21] The Omnibus Budget Reconciliation Act of 1981 redefined the IUR to remove UC exhaustees and EB beneficiaries from the numerator. The Act also eliminated the national IUR trigger, and raised the states' trigger to 5%.

[22] The benefit year is a one-year period during which a worker may receive benefits based on a previous period of unemployment. In all states, the beginning date of the benefit year depends on when a worker first files a valid claim, meaning the worker meets minimal wage and employment requirements.

[23] States would once again be responsible for 50% of the cost of new entrants to the EB benefit program after November 30, 2010, however, as 100% federal financing of the EB plan ends. The federal government would continue to pay 100% of EB benefits for individuals who were receiving EB during the week ending before November 30, 2010, for the duration of their EB receipt.

[24] States that do not require a one-week UC waiting period, or have an exception for any reason to the waiting period, pay 100% of the first week of EB. Twenty-five states, including Rhode Island and North Carolina, do not require a one- week UC waiting period in all cases. P.L. 110-449 (as amended by P.L. 111-5, P.L. 111-118, P.L. 111-144, and P.L. 111-157) suspends this requirement.

[25] For more information on short-time compensation, see CRS Report R40689, *Compensated Work Sharing Arrangements (Short-Time Compensation) as an Alternative to Layoffs*, by Alison M. Shelton.

[26] Senate Committee on Finance Hearing on "Using Unemployment Insurance to Help Americans Get Back to Work: Creating Opportunities and Overcoming Challenges," held on April 14, 2010 (Member statements and witness testimony available: http://finance.senate.gov/hearings/hearing/?id=868a8e37-5056-a032-5297-a991437cea80); House Subcommittee on Income Security and Family Support Hearing on "Responding to Long-Term Unemployment," held June 20, 2010 (Member statements and witness testimony available: http://waysandmeans.house.gov/Hearings/ hearingDetails.aspx?NewsID=1 1201).

[27] U.S. Department of Labor, "Employment Situation Summary," Table A-12, July 2, 2010.

[28] For more information on long-term unemployment, see CRS Report R41 179, *Long-Term Unemployment and Recessions*, by Gerald Mayer and Linda Levine.

[29] For more information on STC, see CRS Report R40689, *Compensated Work Sharing Arrangements (Short-Time Compensation) as an Alternative to Layoffs*, by Alison M. Shelton.

[30] For instance, S. 1646, the Keep Americans Working Act (and its House companion bill, H.R. 4135); S. 2831, the Helping Unemployed Workers Act (and its House companion bill H.R. 4183); H.R. 4179, the SHARE Credit Act of 2009.

[31] For information on job creation strategies in prior recessions, see CRS Report RL31138, *Countercyclical Job Creation Programs of the Post-World War II Era*, by Linda Levine.

[32] For more information on SEA, see CRS Report R41253, *The Self-Employment Assistance (SEA) Program*, by Katelin P. Isaacs

[33] Senate Finance Committee Hearing on "Using Unemployment Insurance to Help Americans Get Back to Work: Creating Opportunities and Overcoming Challenges, held April 14, 2010 (Member statements and witness testimony available: *http://finance.senate.gov/hearings/hearing/?id=868a8e37-5056-a032-5297-a991437cea80).*

[34] See witness testimony from the House Subcommittee on Income Security and Family Support Hearing on "Responding to Long-Term Unemployment," held June 20, 2010 (Member statements and witness testimony available: *http://waysandmeans.house.gov/Hearings/hearingDetails.aspx?NewsID=11201).*

[35] For more information in the TANF ECF, see CRS Report R41078, *The TANF Emergency Contingency Fund*, by Gene Falk.

[36] For additional information on unemployment provisions in the 2009 stimulus package, please see CRS Report R40368, *Unemployment Insurance Provisions in the American Recovery and Reinvestment Act of 2009*, by Alison M. Shelton and Julie M. Whittaker.

[37] For information on short-time compensation programs see CRS Report R40689, *Compensated Work Sharing Arrangements (Short-Time Compensation) as an Alternative to Layoffs*, by Alison M. Shelton.

In: Unemployment: A Closer Look
Editors: Jacob S. Mlakar
ISBN: 978-1-61122-762-8

Chapter 2

UNEMPLOYMENT: ISSUES AND POLICIES

Jane G. Gravelle, Thomas L. Hungerford and Marc Labonte

SUMMARY

The National Bureau of Economic Research (NBER) has declared the U.S. economy to be in recession since December 2007. The unemployment rate in December 2007 was 4.9%; by October 2009, the unemployment rate was above 10%. Although economic output began to grow in the third quarter of 2009, as expected the labor market remained weak into 2010. In response to high unemployment, some Members of Congress proposed job creation bills, following several policy steps taken since the economy entered the recession, including stimulus bills in 2008 (P.L. 110-185) and 2009 (P.L. 111-5), an unprecedented expansion in direct assistance to the financial sector by the Federal Reserve, and the Troubled Asset Relief Program (TARP; P.L. 110-343).

President Obama proposed an additional stimulus package, including tax and other benefits for small business, infrastructure investments, incentives to promote energy efficiency, an extension of benefits for the unemployed, aid to state and local governments, and emergency assistance. The Jobs for Main Street Act of 2009 (H.R. 2847) passed the House on December 16, 2009, and included an extension in unemployment insurance benefits and Consolidated Omnibus Budget Reconciliation Act (COBRA) health benefits, aid to troubled

U.S. states and small businesses, and an increase in infrastructure spending. Some policy analysts have proposed hiring subsidies. The Senate is considering stimulus proposals, including a bill (S.Amdt. 3310 to H.R. 2847) passed on February 24, 2010, to provide job tax credits, an extension in expensing for small business, and an extension of highway funding. A similar bill passed the House on March 4 and was signed by the President (P.L. 111-147) on March 18. The Senate passed H.R. 4213 on March 10, which included extensions in unemployment and health benefits, among other provisions; the House passed a version on Mary 28 that included an extension of unemployment benefits.

Most of the proposals discussed as part of a potential additional macroeconomic jobs bill are traditional fiscal stimulus policies. That is, their objective is to increase total spending (aggregate demand) either through direct spending on programs or by providing funds to others that they will spend (through tax cuts, transfer payments, and aid to state and local governments). Fiscal stimulus is only effective when the policy options actually increase aggregate demand.

Some argue that job tax credits are different from traditional fiscal policies in that their objective is to directly increase employment through a subsidy to labor costs. Studies that examined the 1977-1978 jobs tax credit found mixed results—some conclude that the tax credit was responsible for creating a significant number of jobs, while others conclude that it was ineffective.

The choice of financing affects both the macroeconomic impact and the cost-benefit tradeoff of the policy proposal. Policy measures can be financed by cutting other spending, raising other taxes, or increasing the budget deficit. Economic theory indicates that a deficit-financed policy proposal would have the maximum impact on employment in the short term. Policy changes that increase the deficit, however, move the budget further from long-term sustainability.

Some policymakers have proposed redirecting funds under TARP to finance job creation proposals. Proposals to redirect TARP funds to finance job creation proposals in essence pay for those proposals by reducing the amount that the Treasury Secretary is authorized to purchase under TARP by the cost of the proposal. Since TARP is not near that ceiling today, any proposal that reduces TARP authority by less than $150 billion would not force TARP to be reduced from its currently planned size. Therefore, it would cause the actual budget deficit to increase from the current deficit by the size of the job creation proposal.

In response to high unemployment, some Members of Congress have proposed a job creation bill. This follows several policy steps taken since the economy entered a recession in December 2007, including stimulus bills in 2008 (P.L. 110-185) and 2009 (P.L. 111-5), an unprecedented expansion in direct assistance to the financial sector by the Federal Reserve, and the creation of the Troubled Asset Relief Program (TARP; P.L. 110-343).

President Obama, in a speech on December 8, 2009, proposed an additional stimulus package. This package would include tax and other benefits for small business, infrastructure investments, incentives to promote energy efficiency, and an extension of measures provided in the 2009 legislation with respect to benefits for the unemployed, aid to state and local governments, and emergency assistance. H.R. 2847, the Jobs for Main Street Act of 2009, passed the House on December 16, 2009. It included an extension in unemployment insurance benefits and COBRA health benefits, aid to troubled U.S. states and small businesses, and an increase in infrastructure spending. Some policy analysts have proposed hiring subsidies. The Senate is considering stimulus proposals, including a bill (S.Amdt. 3310 to H.R. 2847) passed on February 24, 2010, to provide job tax credits, an extension in expensing for small business, and an extension of highway funding. A similar bill passed the House on March 4 and the legislation was signed by the President (P.L. 111-147) on March 18. The Senate passed H.R. 4213 on March 10, which included extensions in unemployment and health benefits, among other provisions. The House passed a version of H.R. 4213 on May 28, 2010, that included an extension of unemployment (but not health) benefits.

This report discusses the current unemployment outlook, and analyzes policy proposals to address the issue and options for financing proposals.

THE UNEMPLOYMENT PROBLEM

At the onset of the recession in December 2007, the unemployment rate climbed steadily from a rate of 4.9%, topping 10% in October 2009. This marked the first time since 1982 that unemployment topped 10%; prior to that, unemployment had not topped 10% since the Great Depression. (The rate dropped to 9.7% in January 2010 and remained there in February and March., then rose to 9.9% in April, returning to 0.7% in May.) This recession has been characterized by the biggest percentage point increase in the unemployment rate of any recession since World War II. The duration of unemployment has also been rising. Since mid-2009, over half of those unemployed had been so for 15 weeks or longer. While long-term unemployment has consistently trended upward in past recessions since 1970, the number of long-term unemployed workers has been greater in absolute terms in this recession.

The rise in unemployment has been driven by a steady decline in employment. The decline in employment during this recession can be separated into three phases. From January to August 2008, employment fell between 72,000 and 175,000 per month. From September 2008 to July 2009, employment fell between 304,000 and 741,000 per month. Since July 2009, job losses have tapered off.[1] Nevertheless, employment has continued to fall in every month since December 2007, except for a small increase in November 2009.

Economic output tends to reach its trough and begin growing again before employment. **Figure 1** illustrates that employment has typically begun a sustained increase within four months after the recession has ended, but in the last two "jobless recoveries," employment did not start rising for 12 and 22 months, respectively. The atypical performance of employment in the last two recoveries has at least two possible explanations. First, it may point to fundamental changes in the labor market that could have bearing on job creation in this recovery. Alternatively, it may point to the fact that short and shallow recessions such as the previous two are more likely to have initially weak recoveries, which suggests that a jobless recovery is unlikely to be repeated this time around.

A "hands off" policy approach would counsel for patience—the fall in unemployment will be gradual, but it is also inevitable. Every recession since World War II except the 1980 recession was followed by a period of sustained job creation.[2] As **Figure 1** indicates, although sustained job creation usually happens quickly, employment growth occurred with a long lag after the last two recessions. In the third quarter of 2009, economic output began to grow again. If the economy continues to grow, unemployment will eventually begin to decline. Many economists are projecting that unemployment will peak in mid-2010, and then begin to slowly fall.[3] Historical experience confirms that strong economic growth is the most important factor for reducing unemployment after a recession.[4] Nevertheless, because the unemployment rate is so high, even if the economy grew at a healthy rate, it would take a significant amount of time for unemployment to reach more normal levels. For example, after the unemployment rate peaked at 10.8% in December 1982, the unemployment rate was 8.3% one year later, and it took almost five years for the rate to fall by half. This gradual decline happened over a five-year period when economic growth averaged an unusually high rate of 4.5% annually.

Another argument in favor of patience is that the government has already taken extraordinary steps to stabilize the economy through the creation of the Troubled Asset Relief Program (TARP), the Federal Reserve's emergency lending facilities, and fiscal stimulus in 2008 and 2009, the latter of which contains significant outlays through 2011. These programs will be discussed in greater detail in the following section, entitled "Policy Steps Taken Through 2009." The full economic effects of these previous policy steps will take time to be felt. Proponents of this approach are likely to argue that, with these policies already in place, it is unlikely that further policy steps could sharply hasten the anticipated decline in unemployment.

A more interventionist policy approach could be justified on at least two grounds. First, the loss in output caused by high unemployment is very costly in economic and non-economic terms in the short run. If policy steps to reduce unemployment can be taken at relatively low costs, then the cost-benefit tradeoff would be favorable. A major policy debate at this time, discussed below in the section entitled "Issues in Financing Job Creation Proposals," focuses on just how costly financing these additional policy steps would be.

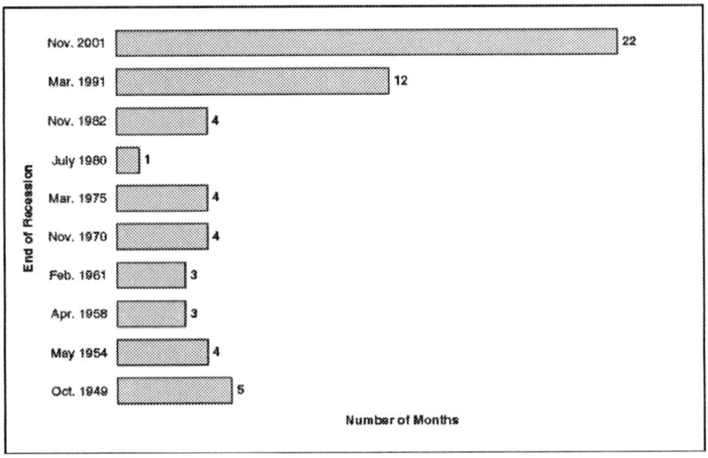

Source: CRS Report R40798, *Unemployment and Employment Trends Before and After the End of Recessions*, by Linda Levine, based on data from the Bureau of Labor Statistics jobs data and Business Cycle Dating Committee for end date of recessions.

Figure 1. Number of Months Into Recovery When Sustained Job Growth Began

The second rationale depends on whether high unemployment has any permanent effects. Mainstream economic theory suggests that the business cycle has no lasting effect on the *natural rate of unemployment*—booms and busts temporarily move the unemployment rate, but it always gravitates back toward its long-term equilibrium rate. In this view, policy steps could hasten the return to the natural rate, but market forces would eventually have caused unemployment to return to the same long-run level on its own. In other words, policy steps would result in temporary (but not permanent) improvements in well-being. Some economists have offered a competing theory called "hysteresis," however. In this view, bouts of high unemployment can lead to permanent increases in the natural rate of unemployment, so that unemployment never falls as low in the subsequent recovery as it had been at the previous peak. This theory was developed to explain the failure of high unemployment to fall in Western Europe in the 1980s expansion.[5] Hysteresis could result from imperfections in labor markets or from workers losing some of their skills in long bouts of unemployment that reduce their subsequent employability. If hysteresis effects are significant, then policy steps that successfully reduce unemployment now could avoid some permanent loss in well-being.

POLICY STEPS TAKEN THROUGH 2009

The National Bureau of Economic Research (NBER) declared the U.S. economy to be in recession since December 2007. Numerous actions have already been taken to contain damages spilling over from housing and financial markets to the broader economy. These policies include traditional monetary and fiscal policy, as well as federal interventions into the financial sector.

In February 2008, in response to weaker economic growth, an economic stimulus package of approximately $150 billion was adopted.[6] A provision that was considered (but not enacted) in the February stimulus bill was a 26-week extension of unemployment benefits; this extension was eventually enacted.[7]

With the worsening performance of the economy, congressional leaders and President Obama proposed much larger stimulus packages at the beginning of 2009. The American Recovery and Reinvestment Act of 2009 (ARRA), an $820 billion package with $275 billion in tax cuts (offset by a $7 billion gain from the treatment of built-in losses) and the remainder in spending, was passed by the House on January 28 (H.R. 1). It was a wide-ranging package that included infrastructure spending, revenue sharing with the states, middle class tax cuts, business tax cuts, unemployment benefits, and food stamps. Similar legislation was passed in the Senate on February 10 (an amendment in the nature of a substitute for H.R. 1) and would cost $838 billion, with $292 billion in tax cuts. The version of the bill signed into law on February 17, 2009 (P.L. 111-5), was a $787 billion package with $286 billion in tax cuts and the remainder in spending.[8] The largest budgetary effects of P.L. 111-5 occur in FY20 10 (equaling 2.2% of GDP, compared with 1.3% in 2009), so this legislation has not yet had its peak effect on the economy.

A number of financial-sector interventions have also been undertaken, before and after financial market conditions worsened significantly in September 2008. The Federal Reserve (Fed) has reduced short-term interest rates to zero and introduced a number of facilities, providing direct assistance to the financial system that would eventually surpass $1 trillion. In October 2008, legislation was enacted granting the Treasury Department authority to purchase up to $700 billion in assets through TARP.[9] A number of programs have been created under TARP, including programs to inject capital into banks, aid automakers and troubled financial firms, and modify mortgages. The Federal Reserve is close to completing purchases of $1.25 billion of mortgage- backed securities, $175 billion in Government-Sponsored Enterprise (GSE) debt, and $300 billion of long-term Treasury debt. On March 23, 2009, the Treasury announced a plan for a public- private partnership to purchase troubled assets, including one part that uses the Federal Deposit Insurance Corporation (FDIC) to insure loans and another part that would allow access to the Federal Reserve's Term Asset-Backed Securities Loan Facility (TALF).[10] Other policies enacted in response to the financial crisis include an FDIC guarantee of debt issued by banks, a Treasury guarantee of money market mutual funds, and Treasury support of the GSEs.

Policy Proposals

In December 2009, the House passed H.R. 2847, which extends unemployment benefits, food stamps, and Medicare and COBRA health benefits, and provides additional funds for infrastructure and aid to state and local governments (details below). The Senate Leadership proposed a jobs bill early in 2010. President Obama, in a speech on December 8, 2009, proposed an additional stimulus package to include tax and other benefits for small business (including incentives for hiring), infrastructure investments, incentives to promote energy efficiency, and an extension of relief provided in the 2009 legislation for benefits for the unemployed, state aid, and emergency assistance. Proposals have also been circulating for some time to provide an incremental jobs tax credit.

The House passed H.R. 4691 on February 25, a separate measured providing for a short term extension of a number of provisions about to expire, including expanded unemployment insurance and COBRA health benefits, certain Medicare provisions, use of the 2009 poverty guidelines for means-tested programs, and extensions of small business loans. Overall, the 10- year cost is $10.3 billion, with most of the cost occurring in FY2010.[11] The Senate is considering an extension as well.

The Senate passed an amendment to H.R. 2847, S.Amdt. 3310, on February 24, 2010 (see discussion under "Senate Proposals"), which included a jobs credit. The House passed a similar version on March 4, 2010, and the President signed the legislation (P.L. 111-147) on March 18, 2010.

Both the House and Senate recently passed emergency extensions of certain unemployment and health benefits.

The Senate on March 10 passed H.R. 4213 (see discussion under "Senate Proposals"), which included extensions of unemployment, health and other benefits, along with other tax and spending provisions not specifically directed at stimulus. The House passed its version of H.R. 4213 on May 28.

December 2009 House Proposal (H.R. 2847)

On December 16, the House passed the Jobs for Main Street Act of 2010, H.R. 2847. This bill provided for $154 billion in spending, allocated to three categories: infrastructure spending, public service jobs, and emergency funding (see **Figure 2**). The last category includes a tax cut. The proposal redirects TARP funds to finance the spending. [12] The bill also provides for an extension of the surface transportation authorization through the fiscal year and an extension of the statute of limitations for claims of discrimination in USDA's credit programs and provides funding for remedies.

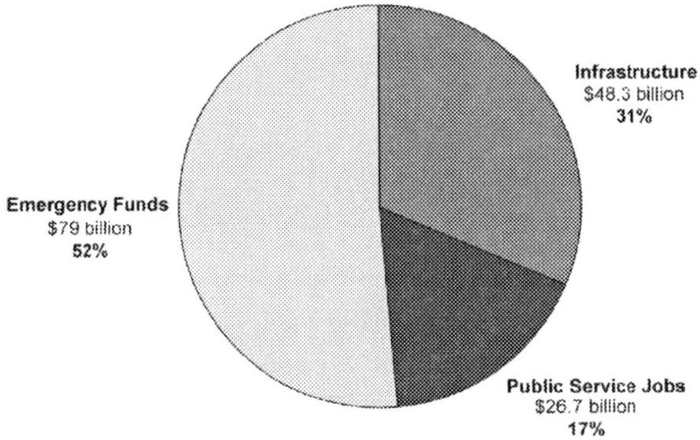

Source: CRS.

Figure 2. Distribution of Spending Under the Jobs for Main Street Act (H.R. 2847)

Infrastructure Spending

The proposal allots $48.3 billion (31% of the total) for additional infrastructure spending. About three-quarters of the infrastructure spending is for surface transportation (57% or $27.5 billion for highways, 17% or $8.4 billion for mass transit, and 1.7% or $800 million for Amtrak). The transit funds include $6.15 billion for urban and rural formula grants, $500 million for capital investment grants for new or expanded fixed highway projects, and $1.75 billion in formula grants for repair. The Amtrak funds are capital grants. Other transportation projects include $500 million for airports improvement and $100 million for the Maritime Guaranteed Loan program.

Slightly over 8% of the infrastructure total ($4.1 billion) is allocated to school renovation grants. About 6% ($2.8 billion) is allocated to environmental, flood, and similar spending: $2 billion for clean water ($1 billion for the Clean Water State Revolving Fund and $1 billion for the Safe Water Drinking Fund), $100 million for the Bureau of Reclamation to provide water in rural areas, and $0.7 15 billion for Corps of Engineers projects. The proposal also includes $2 billion for the Department of Energy Innovation Technology Loan Guarantee program for renewable energy, $1 billion for the National Housing Trust Fund to provide low-income rental housing, along with $65 million in vouchers, and $1 billion for repair and rehabilitation of public housing.

Public Service Jobs

The bill provides for $26.7 billion in funding (17% of the total) for public service jobs, with the bulk of funds ($23 billion, or 86% of the total in this category) for education. About 95% of these funds would be allocated to school districts and public institutions of higher learning, to retain or create jobs for teachers and other educational services and to modernize and repair facilities. The remaining 5% will be allocated to the states. The plan also provides funds to support law enforcement jobs ($1.18 billion) and firefighter jobs ($0.5 billion).

The bill also provides the following amounts to support other types of jobs: $200 million for Americorps, $500 million for summer youth employment, $300 million for the college work study program, $270 million for parts and forestry workers, and $750 million for competitive grants to support job training in high-growth and emerging industry, particularly health care and green industries.

Emergency Funding

Over half of the total funds, $79 billion, would be directed at relief provisions. Almost all of this category (97%) is directed at three programs: a six-month extension of expanded unemployment benefits ($41 billion, or 52%), a six-month extension of the higher Medicaid match for doctors payments ($23.5 billion, or 30%), and an extension from nine to 15 months of the subsidy for health insurance for unemployed workers ($12.3 billion or 16%) under COBRA. The package also includes $2.3 billion to increase the eligibility for refundability of the child tax credit. This latter provision would remove the $3,000 floor that occurs before the child credit can become refundable. The plan also provides $354 million to continue Small Business Administration temporary loan authority guarantees through FY2010 and $305 million to freeze Department of Health and Human Services (HHS) poverty guidelines at 2009 levels to prevent a reduction in a variety of means-tested benefits. The bill also contains two provisions with negligible revenue cost: a provision that individuals may exclude tax refunds for assessing eligibility for means- tested programs for a year, and a provision for legal assistance to Social Security and Supplemental Security Income disability claimants.

Senate Proposals

On February 24, the Senate adopted S.Amdt. 3310 to H.R. 2847 (Hiring Incentives to Restore Employment), which includes payroll tax credits equal to the employer's share of OASDI (payroll taxes of 6.2% that finance Social Security) for hiring those who have been unemployed for at least 60 days and a $1,000 income tax credit for these employees once they have been retained for 52 weeks. This provision is the principal one, in dollar amounts, of the package, costing $13 billion , with $7.6 billion for the payroll relief and $5.3 billion for the retention credit. All cost estimates reported in this section are over 10 years, although the costs for the credit will occur in 2010 and 2011.[13] Other provisions include an option to convert tax credit bonds to Build America Bonds ($2.5 billion), an extension in the small business expensing provision through 2010 ($35 million), and an extension of the highway bill that provides transfers between the general funds and trust funds. S.Amdt. 3310 also contains offsets relating to foreign tax compliance (a gain of $8.7 billion)[14] and a further two-year delay in the worldwide interest allocation for the foreign tax credit ($7.9 billion). [15] As noted above, the House passed the bill as well and it was signed by the President on March 18, 2010 (P.L. 111-147).

The Senate is also considering H.R. 4691, the bill passed by the House to provide a short-term extension of certain programs.

Except for the interest allocation provision, the provisions in S.Amdt. 3310 were contained in a larger package proposed by Chairman Baucus and Ranking Member Grassley of the Senate Finance Committee.[16] Other provisions are scheduled to be considered in subsequent legislation, although not all would necessarily be considered in the nature of stimulus provisions. One component is addressing the extenders, a number of temporary tax provisions that generally are extended each year, and cost $31 billion.

Other stimulus provisions in the package included an extension of unemployment insurance ($22 billion) and COBRA health insurance subsidies ($3 billion). The package also includes $10 billion for extending health provisions including delaying reduction in Medicare payments, other health spending, and retaining the 2009 poverty guidelines to prevent individuals from losing means-tested benefits. It also allows for a disregard of refundable tax credits and refunds for these means-tested programs.

The proposal includes $3 billion in extensions of provisions not under the jurisdiction of the Finance Committee: expiring authorities under the Patriot Act, flood insurance, small business loans, agricultural disaster assistance (accounting for $1.5 billion of the $3 billion total), and satellite home viewer legislation.

Offsets, other than the foreign compliance provisions included in S.Amdt. 3310, include a $24 billion cellulosic biofuels provision primarily aimed at reducing eligibility of "black liquor" (a by-product of paper manufacturing) for tax credits, a clarification of the economic substance doctrine and increased penalties for transactions without substance ($5 billion),[17] and an $8 billion reduction in the Medicare improvement fund. In addition to specified offsets, the plan would reduce the requirement for employers, whose assets have declined in value, to contribute additional funds to pension plans, saving $6 billion in revenues (because of reduced deductions).

On March 10, the Senate passed its version of H.R. 4213, the American Workers, State and Business Relief Act, which provided $59 billion for an extension of unemployment benefits, $29 billion for health provisions including an extension of COBRA health benefits for unemployed workers, an extension for Medicaid funding and reversing a reduction in payments for doctors, and $2 billion for other purposes (poverty guidelines and disregards for means tested programs). This bill also included extenders and offsets not related to stimulus objectives.

On May 28, the House passed its version of H.R. 4213, the American Jobs and Closing Loopholes Act. It included $41 billion of additional spending for unemployment compensation, some smaller spending provisions of $10 billion, and some provisions relating to Medicare payments for physicians, along with tax extenders and some other tax provisions largely unrelated to short-run stimulus.

President Obama's Proposal

In a speech at the Brookings Institution on October 8, 2009, President Obama proposed a four- part stimulus plan. [18] The plan includes the general elements in the House plan and some additional proposals. Subsequent details of these proposals have been announced in the budget documents[19] and in a White House fact sheet on the jobs credit.[20]

The first part of the plan would provide tax benefits and loans to small businesses. The proposal would provide a $5,000 credit for each net new employee and a forgiveness of payroll taxes for any increases in payroll. These provisions are offset against the payroll tax, and thus available quarterly, and are available to nonprofits (start up firms get half the credit). The credit is capped at $500,000. The plan would also extend a provision to allow increased expensing for equipment purchases by small businesses, enacted in the 2009 stimulus bill for 2009 through 2010. Under the increased expensing provision, firms may deduct up to $250,000 of the cost of equipment, with a phaseout beginning at $800,000.[21] The plan would also completely exempt capital gains on small business stock. This provision has a relatively small revenue effect.[22]

The small business proposals also include plans to use remaining TARP funding for small business loans, which could be done without congressional action.

The second part of the proposal is an increase in infrastructure spending, to extend further into the future than the spending authorized in the 2009 stimulus.

The third part of the proposal is to provide incentives for individuals to retrofit homes for energy efficiency and to expand other initiatives in the 2009 stimulus to promote energy efficiency and clean-energy jobs.

The final part of the proposal is to extend relief in the 2009 stimulus, including emergency assistance to seniors, unemployment insurance benefits, COBRA health benefits for those who have lost their health insurance, and relief to state and local governments to prevent layoffs.

The President also indicated support of the House bill, H.R. 2847, as a complement to his plans, in a statement released on December 16, 2009.[23]

Incremental Jobs Tax Credit

A proposal that has been circulating for some time, and that might be considered as a small business hiring incentive, is an incremental jobs tax credit. Variations of these credits are in the Senate proposal and in President Obama's proposal.[24] This type of credit would provide benefits for hiring employees in excess of a base amount. The United States had one historical experience with this type of credit in 1977 and 1978 (the New Jobs Tax Credit).[25] The tax code has contained for some time permanent tax credits targeted at certain types of workers, and the target groups were expanded somewhat in 2009.[26] These credits are applicable to newly hired workers from the targeted groups without requiring an increase in a firm's total employment, however.

Discussion

Both monetary and fiscal policy can be used to stimulate the economy. The proposals addressed above include direct spending by the government, transfers to state and local governments (for either infrastructure spending, Medicare, or other purposes), direct transfers to individuals (such as unemployment compensation), tax cuts for individuals, and tax incentives aimed at businesses, including jobs tax credits. Jobs subsidies differ from policies aimed at increasing aggregate demand, in that they are supply-side subsidies. That is, the initial effect is not aimed at inducing spending that will then encourage firms to expand output and hire workers (although it may do so), but is aimed at reducing the cost of hiring workers, so as to induce more hires. The first section below discusses traditional fiscal policies, the second discusses incentives aimed at jobs.

Spending, Transfers, and Tax Cuts

Most of the proposals discussed as part of a potential additional macroeconomic jobs bill are traditional fiscal policies similar to those enacted in 2009. That is, their objective is to increase total spending (aggregate demand) either through direct spending on programs or by providing funds to others that will spend (through transfer payments, tax cuts, and aid to state and local governments). The House bill is composed almost entirely of spending and transfers (with a small tax cut, the increased child credit refundability). President Obama's proposal does not contain details, although it appears that, while much of the proposal involves spending and transfers, part of the proposal will be aimed at tax cuts for small businesses. (This section of the proposal would also include a subsidy for labor, discussed in the next subsection.)

The issues surrounding these fiscal instruments are the same as those relating to the previous stimulus, except that it is later in the business cycle and there is a greater possibility that the provisions may come later than is desirable.[27] Many economists view fiscal policy as less effective than monetary policy in an open economy.[28]

Fiscal stimulus is only effective from a macroeconomic perspective when it increases aggregate demand. The size of the proposal and financing are the most important determinants of its effect on aggregate demand. For example, the House bill is about 1% of output, about the size of the February 2008 stimulus, but considerably smaller than the February 2009 stimulus (which was estimated to be 1.3% of output in 2009 and 2.2% in 2010). As discussed in the section entitled "Issues in Financing Job Creation Proposals," in the standard macroeconomic model, only deficit- financed proposals would have a significant effect on aggregate demand.

Fiscal stimulus can involve tax cuts, spending increases, or a combination of both. Tax cuts may be less effective than spending because some of the tax cut may be saved, which diminishes the effectiveness of the stimulus.[29] Some argue that tax cuts that are temporary, appear in a lump sum rather than in withholding, or are aimed at higher-income individuals are more likely to be saved. [30] Transfer payments are similar to tax cuts, but tend to be received by lower-income individuals who are more likely to spend them. Evidence generally suggests that tax subsidies for business tax cuts are not very effective.[31] Mark Zandi, for example, has suggested that the multipliers (the dollar increase in real output for each dollar of stimulus) for personal tax cuts range between 1 and 1.3, the multipliers for spending and transfer payments range over 1.5, and multipliers for transfers to state and local governments range under 1.5.[32]

The challenge to spending programs is that there may be a lag time for planning and administration before the money is spent. Some analysts suggest that aid to state and local governments may be spent more quickly because these governments are likely to cut back on spending in downturns due to balanced budget requirements, and the aid may forestall these cuts. Extending ARRA infrastructure spending is unlikely to be spent quickly since all the spending under ARRA has not occurred yet. The receipt of tax cuts can also be delayed, if they are delivered through changes to withholding or through a delayed refund. If a stimulus is considered or enacted as the economy is beginning to recover, its benefits may be limited given these lags.

Subsidies to business investment are, like other policies, aimed at increasing aggregate demand (through increased investment spending). The small business investment subsidies suffer from the same problems confronting business subsidies for investment in general, namely, although in theory a temporary subsidy should be the most effective investment stimulus, evidence from prior investment subsidies does not suggest that such subsidies are very effective. [33] The lack of effectiveness may occur in part because businesses with losses cannot take advantage of the provision and in part because firms may already have excess capacity. The extension of the expensing provision for small business, however, has mixed effects because firms in the phaseout range have a marginal disincentive to invest. In any case, the potential effect on spending is limited by the fact that these provisions are relatively small in revenue effect.

Job Credits

Some argue the job credit provisions are different from traditional fiscal policies in that their objective is to directly increase employment through a subsidy to labor costs. A general subsidy to labor (such as a forgiveness of the employer's share of payroll taxes) would be relatively costly. (In the short run, a forgiveness of the employee's share would be similar to an individual income tax cut while forgiveness of the employer's share would be similar to a job credit.)

More research has been done on an incremental job tax credit, which was a policy adopted in 1977 and 1978. Two proponents of this policy, Bartik and Bishop, have argued that the proposal will be successful in creating a significant number of jobs.[34] Their estimates were done by assuming a labor demand elasticity of 0.3, which indicates that a 10% reduction in the cost of labor would increase employment by 3%. Note that their estimates did not rest on a study of the 1977-78 credit, but rather predicted the effect on jobs based on a central tendency labor demand elasticity.[35] Note that this estimate is a general demand elasticity, and might not necessarily be as high during a recession, when business is slack.

Studies that examined the 1977-1978 credit found mixed results. Bishop studied the construction, retailing, and wholesaling industries, accounting for the effect of the jobs credit, and found that the credit was responsible for 150,000 to 600,000 of the 1 million increase in employment during that period. [36] Perloff and Wachter compared firms who knew about the credit with those who did not and found employment growth to be greater among the former group, although they caution that this is not a random selection and there may be characteristics about firms with more knowledge that could independently affect growth. Overall, they seem to conclude that the credit did not work very well because many firms were not aware of it, and many firms did not have enough employment growth.[37] Tannenwald surveyed Wisconsin and New England firms.[38] He found that the effect was smaller than predicted. He indicated that most estimates of the labor demand response to a change in wages indicate that a 10% change in wages lead to labor demand increases of 2%. These estimates are general estimates, not associated with a downturn. He found an increase of only 0.4%, less than a quarter of the projected effects. The major reason was the lack of product demand. For example, one quote from his survey was: "Orders determine levels of hiring, not tax gimmicks." The main reservation about a jobs tax credit is that it might not be effective in those industries that are experiencing slack demand, causing the labor demand elasticity, already low in normal times, to approach a very low level.[39]

While an incremental credit can have a larger "bang for the buck" by only providing subsidies for additional hiring, it is also much more complicated and can possibly be evaded (for example, firms may hire their contractors temporarily). The 1977-1978 credit was made incremental in Congress (presumably to increase bang for the buck), but an incremental subsidy was opposed by the Carter Administration because of complexity and unfairness. Sunley discusses a variety of distortions that arise from an incremental credit, depending on the design, such as hiring part-time workers instead of full-time, reducing overtime, and hiring and replacing workers. Also, it automatically favors firms that are growing anyway, which leads to geographic differentials.[40]

ISSUES IN FINANCING JOB CREATION PROPOSALS

Another consideration is how to finance any proposed policy measure. The choice of financing affects both the macroeconomic impact and the cost-benefit tradeoff of the policy proposal. Policy measures can be financed by cutting other spending, raising other taxes, or increasing the budget deficit.

Economic theory indicates that a deficit-financed policy proposal would have the maximum impact on employment in the short term. In a deep recession, total spending (aggregate demand) in the economy is inadequate to fully employ labor and capital resources. In other words, lack of aggregate demand is the main cause of high unemployment. Increasing the budget deficit can increase total spending in the economy and bring some of those idle resources back into use. Deficit-neutral proposals would tend to neutralize the effects of job creation provisions on total spending in the economy by cutting other spending or lowering the spending of those whose taxes are raised. Deficit-neutral policies can be used to lower the cost of labor, but without any increase in demand for their products, employers may be unresponsive to incentives to increase their labor force.

In the context of a deep recession, the short-term economic cost of increasing the budget deficit may be quite low. The main economic costs of increasing the deficit come from its tendency to "crowd out" private investment spending or increase the trade deficit.[41] Deficits crowd out private investment spending because their financing requires scarce private saving. Increasing the demands on this private saving raises interest rates, making private investment spending less attractive. In the current context, investment spending has been greatly reduced by the recession, so there is less chance of it being crowded out by the larger deficit in the short run. Unusually low Treasury bond rates are evidence that the crowding out factor is not significant at present.[42] Deficits and domestic private investment spending can also be financed through foreign capital flows, however. An increase in net foreign capital inflows must be matched by an equal increase in the trade deficit.[43] With perfect capital mobility, the stimulus to total spending caused by the larger deficit could be entirely offset by the decline in total spending resulting from a larger trade deficit. Since the trade deficit has fallen significantly since the beginning of 2007, this drawback to increasing the deficit may also be less important at present.

While an economic argument can be made that increasing the deficit could have short-term benefits, that argument may presuppose that the increase in the deficit would be reversed when economic conditions return to normal. Political constraints may make that difficult, and could lead one to conclude that the short-term benefits of higher deficits would be outweighed by the long-term costs—namely, that if deficits are not reduced when unemployment falls, the effects on investment spending and the trade deficit would become greater. Indeed, any proposal to increase the deficit can be viewed in the broader context of an overall deficit that in 2009 was larger relative to the size of the economy than all but a handful of previous wartime years. The 2009 deficit is not sustainable in the long run in the sense that deficits of that size would cause the national debt to continually rise relative to output. A deficit of this size cannot be maintained indefinitely without eventually resulting in a fiscal crisis where investors refuse to continue financing it because they no longer believe that the government would be capable of servicing it. While there is no sign of investor unwillingness to hold federal debt at the present (since borrowing rates are so low), it is also difficult to predict at what point investors would refuse to hold more debt. Essentially, investors are willing to hold federal debt as long as they believe that the government will eventually reduce the deficit to the point where it becomes sustainable. Policy changes that increase the deficit place the deficit further from sustainability.[44]

Redirecting TARP Funds to Finance Proposals

Some policymakers have proposed redirecting funds under TARP to finance job creation proposals. H.R. 2847, which passed the House on December 16, 2009, redirected $150 billion of TARP funds to finance the bill's other provisions. Under the Emergency Economic Stabilization Act (Division A of H.R. 1424/P.L. 110-343), Congress authorized up to $700 billion to be outstanding for the life of the program to purchase "troubled assets," as defined by the Treasury Secretary. In its November 2009 monthly report to Congress, Treasury reported that $550 billion of TARP expenditures had been planned and $476 billion had been committed under signed contracts, signifying that Treasury has no plans at this time to use $150 billion of the funds authorized.[45] Treasury's planned use of available TARP funds can change at any time, however.

When TARP was created, the Treasury did not collect and set aside $700 billion of revenue to finance the program—the Treasury Secretary was simply given legal authority to purchase $700 billion of assets. Therefore, Treasury holds no unused money under TARP that can be redirected toward new policy proposals. Like most spending programs, TARP expenditures are financed from general revenues. When the budget is in deficit, additional expenditures are financed by additional borrowing. If the Treasury Secretary wished to purchase more TARP assets, it would be necessary to first issue federal debt (thereby increasing the budget deficit) to do so. The size of the actual deficit today is based on the cost of TARP expenditures taken during this fiscal year (the method for measuring the cost is described below); the projected size of the future deficit in budget projections is based on some assumption about how much the Treasury Secretary plans to increase the size of TARP in the future and how much these future expenditures will cost.

Proposals to redirect TARP funds to finance job creation policies rely, in essence, on a reduction in the amount that the Treasury Secretary is authorized to purchase under TARP. Since TARP is not near its ceiling today, any proposal that reduces TARP authority by less than $150 billion would not force TARP asset holdings to be reduced from the currently planned size. Thus, reducing the authorized size of TARP by less than $150 billion does not increase the revenues flowing to the Treasury because it does not force Treasury to sell any of the assets TARP currently holds. In effect, a new policy proposal that increases spending or reduces revenues would be deficit-financed if it included a reduction in TARP authority of less than $150 billion under Treasury's current plan (since it would not result in any increase in revenues via a reduction in TARP assets outstanding).

A separate issue is whether redirecting TARP funds to finance job creation proposals would increase the expected budget deficit in the future compared to projections of current policy. This measure would be relevant for scoring the proposal and for measuring the proposal's macroeconomic effects relative to a baseline of current policy. The answer to this question depends on what assumption is made about the future size of the TARP program under current policy baselines, which need not be the same as Treasury's announced plans since those plans are not binding. Through March 2009, the Congressional Budget Office (CBO) baseline assumed that the amount outstanding under TARP would reach $700 billion. In August 2009, CBO modified its baseline and assumed that TARP would peak at $600 billion, or $50 billion higher than Treasury's current plans. That implies that reducing TARP by up to $100 billion would have no impact on future projections of the baseline deficit (because the baseline already assumed that the redirected money would not be spent by TARP), so redirecting TARP by up to that amount to finance a new proposal would be fully matched by an increase in the deficit.[46] From a macroeconomic perspective, a job creation proposal to be financed by a decrease in TARP authority of up to $100 billion would have the same effect on economic projections compared to the August baseline as if it were deficit-financed.

For official scoring purposes in 2009, the 2009 budget resolution (S.Con.Res. 13) instructs CBO to use the March baseline, even though a more recent baseline is now available. (The same baseline is used so that scoring will be consistent throughout the session.) Therefore, a bill financed by redirecting any TARP funds would be officially scored as being offset by a decline in overall anticipated federal spending via a smaller TARP program since the March baseline assumed all $700 billion of TARP authority would be used in the future. The offset would not be one-for-one, however. Under Section 123 of EESA, the cost of asset purchases are scored as the net present value of the subsidy in the loan, modified for risk, and are not scored on a cash flow basis. For future TARP spending, CBO assumes a subsidy rate of 50%. Therefore, a dollar reduction in TARP authority is scored as reducing the official budget deficit by only 50 cents.[47]

End Notes

[1] The data described here are net figures from the Bureau of Labor Statistics' establishment survey. Despite the recession, gross job gains at firms averaged 7 million per quarter in 2008, down from 7.6 million per quarter in 2007. These gross job gains have been more than offset by gross job losses, however. Gross job losses at firms averaged 7.9 million per quarter in 2008, up from 7.4 million per quarter in 2007.

[2] In the case of the 1980 expansion, the economy slid back into recession in 1981.

[3] See *Blue Chip Economic Indicators*, vol. 34, no. 12, December 10, 2009.

[4] See CRS Report R40925, *Unemployment and Economic Recovery*, by Brian W. Cashell.

[5] See Olivier Blanchard and Lawrence Summers, "Hysteresis and the European Unemployment Problem," in Stanley Fischer, ed., *NBER Macroeconomics Annual*, vol. 1 (Cambridge: MIT Press, 1986), p. 15.

[6] A second stimulus plan (H.R. 7110) passed the House on September 26, 2008, but was not passed by the Senate before the 110th Congress ended. It included $36.9 billion on infrastructure ($12.8 billion highway and bridge, $7.5 billion water and sewer, $5 billion

Corps of Engineers); $6.5 billion in extended unemployment compensation; $14.5 billion in Medicaid; and $2.7 billion in food stamp and nutrition programs.

[7] For a discussion of the tax, housing, and unemployment legislation adopted in the 110th Congress, see CRS Report RS22850, *Tax Provisions of the 2008 Economic Stimulus Package*, by Jane G. Gravelle; CRS Report RS22 172, *The Conforming Loan Limit*, by N. Eric Weiss and Mark Jickling; and CRS Report RS22915, *Temporary Extension of Unemployment Benefits: Emergency Unemployment Compensation (EUC08)*, by Katelin P. Isaacs, Julie M. Whittaker, and Alison M. Shelton.

[8] For a discussion of the American Recovery and Reinvestment Act of 2009, see CRS Report R40104, *Economic Stimulus: Issues and Policies*, by Jane G. Gravelle, Thomas L. Hungerford, and Marc Labonte.

[9] See CRS Report RL34427, *Financial Turmoil: Federal Reserve Policy Responses*, by Marc Labonte for a discussion of Federal Reserve Policy, and CRS Report RL34730, *Troubled Asset Relief Program: Legislation and Treasury Implementation*, by Baird Webel and Edward V. Murphy.

[10] For further discussion, see CRS Report RL34730, *Troubled Asset Relief Program: Legislation and Treasury Implementation*, by Baird Webel and Edward V. Murphy.

[11] See estimates at http://www.cbo.gov/ftpdocs/112xx/doc11261/hr4691.pdf.

[12] The estimates presented in this section are taken from Jobs for Mainstreet, posted on Speaker Pelosi's website at http://www.speaker.gov/newsroom/legislation

[13] Cost estimates are at http://www.cbo.gov/ftpdocs/112xx/doc11230/hr2847.pdf and further tax details are included in the Joint Committee on Taxation, JCX-5-10 at http://www.jct.gov/publications.html?func=startdown&id=3649.

[14] These proposals involve a variety of additional information reporting, disclosure, and related penalties associated with foreign banks and trusts, an increase in the statute of limitations for foreign matters, and clarifications regarding foreign trusts and dividend equivalent securities. For general background on matters of individual tax evasion with foreign investments see CRS Report R40623, *Tax Havens: International Tax Avoidance and Evasion*, by Jane G. Gravelle

[15] See CRS Report RL34494, *The Foreign Tax Credit's Interest Allocation Rules*, by Jane G. Gravelle and Donald J. Marples.

[16] Press Release on Hiring Incentives to Restore Employment Act, *http://finance.senate.go v/press/Bpress/2010press/* prb021110a.pdf.

[17] For a brief explanation, see CRS Report RL34249, *The Tax Reduction and Reform Act of 2007: An Overview*, by Jane G. Gravelle.

[18] The proposal is discussed at http://www.whitehouse.gov/the-press-office/president-obama-announces-proposalsaccelerate-job-growth-and-lay-foundation-robust.

[19] See Reviving Job Creation and Laying a Foundation for Economic Growth, http://www.gpoaccess.gov/usbudget/ fy11/pdf/budget/reviving.pdf.

[20] See http://www.whitehouse.gov/sites/default/files/ FACT_SHEET_Small_Business%20jobs_and_Wages_Tax_Cut.pdf.

[21] Currently the allowance is scheduled to drop to $125,000 for 2010, with a phaseout beginning at $500,000. This higher level is itself a temporary provision as part of the 200 1-2003 tax cuts, so that the allowance will fall to $25,000, with a phaseout beginning at $200,000 in 2011.

[22] A provision exempting 50% of the gain on small business stock and taxing the remaining gain at 28% has been in the tax law since 1993, but its relative benefit largely disappeared when capital gains tax rates were reduced to 15%. The 2009 legislation increased the exemption to 75% and the President's proposal would increase it to 100%. See CRS Report R40728, *Small Business Tax Benefits and the American Recovery and Reinvestment Act of 2009*, by Gary Guenther for a discussion.

[23] See http://www.whitehouse.gov/the-press-office/statement-president-house-passage-jobs-bill.

[24] Amore detailed analysis of job tax credits is in CRS Report R41034, *Business Investment and Employment Tax Incentives to Stimulate the Economy*, by Thomas L. Hungerford and Jane G. Gravelle.

[25] See CRS Report 92-93 9, *Countercyclical Job Creation Programs*, by Linda Levine for a discussion.

[26] For more information, see CRS Report RL3 0089, *The Work Opportunity Tax Credit (WOTC)*, by Linda Levine.

[27] See the discussions below addressing the issues of financing the jobs programs from TARP funds, which indicate that this assumption does not change the characterization of stimulus proposals. See CRS Report R40104, *Economic Stimulus: Issues and Policies*, by Jane G. Gravelle, Thomas L. Hungerford, and Marc Labonte for a more extensive discussion of the issues surrounding the 2009 stimulus. See CRS Report RS22790, *Tax Cuts for Short-Run Economic Stimulus: Recent Experiences*, coordinated by Jane G. Gravelle for evidence on the effectiveness of recent policy options.

[28] When fiscal expansion raises the deficit and drives up interest rates, capital is attracted from abroad. The purchase of U.S. dollars by foreigners to buy U.S. assets drives up the price of the dollar, causing export demand to decline. This reduction in the demand for exports offsets in part (perhaps in large part) the initial increase in demand induced by the stimulus. The more mobile international capital flows are the larger offsetting effect.

[29] See CRS Report RS21 136, *Government Spending or Tax Reduction: Which Might Add More Stimulus to the Economy?*, by Marc Labonte.

[30] CRS Report RS21 126, *Tax Cuts and Economic Stimulus: How Effective Are the Alternatives?*, by Jane G. Gravelle.

[31] See CRS Report RL31134, *Using Business Tax Cuts to Stimulate the Economy*, by Jane G. Gravelle.

[32] Mark Zandi, Moody's Economy. com. Also see CRS Report R40 104, *Economic Stimulus: Issues and Policies*, by Jane G. Gravelle, Thomas L. Hungerford, and Marc Labonte for a list of multipliers. This report also discusses the effects of alternative tax and spending policies in more detail.

[33] See CRS Report RL31134, *Using Business Tax Cuts to Stimulate the Economy*, by Jane G. Gravelle.

[34] Timothy J. Bartik and John H. Bishop, *The Job Creation Tax Credit*, Economic Policy Institute Briefing Paper, October 20, 2009, http://www.epi.org/publications/entry/bp248/.

[35] See Daniel L. Hamermesh, *Labor Demand* (Princeton University Press: Princeton, NJ, 1993), for a survey: Hamermesh suggests a midpoint elasticity of 0.3 on p. 92.

[36] John Bishop, "Employment in Construction and Distribution Industries: The Impact of the New Jobs Tax Credit," in *Studies in Labor Markets*, University of Chicago Press, 1981, pp. 209-246.

[37] Jeffrey J. Perloff and Michael L. Walchter, "The New Jobs Tax Credit," *American Economic Review*, vol. 69, May 1989, pp. 173-179.

[38] Robert Tannenwald, "Are Wage and Training Subsidies Cost-Effective? Some Evidence from the New Jobs Tax Credit," *New England Economic Review*, September/October 1982, pp. 25-34.

[39] Although the issues are somewhat different, studies of permanent targeted jobs tax credits that are aimed at disadvantaged workers have generally found limited effects. Daniel L. Hammermesh, *Labor Demand* (Princeton University Press: Princeton, NJ, 1993) reviews the evidence on the effects of several earlier jobs subsidies. For studies of the current work opportunity credit, see CRS Report RL3 0089, *The Work Opportunity Tax Credit (WOTC)*, by Linda Levine.

[40] These positions, as well as problems with the credit, were discussed by a Carter Administration official, Emil Sunley, in "Legislative History of the New Jobs Tax Credit," *The Economics of Taxation*, Edited by Henry J. Aaron and Michael J. Boskin, Washington, DC, The Brookings Institution, 1980. See also James Leigh Griffith, "A Critical View of the

Complexity and Effect of the New Jobs Credit," *The Tax Lawyer*, vol. 32, Fall 1978, pp. 157-179, and Roland L. Hjorth, "New Jobs Credit," *Taxes: The Tax Magazine*, vol. 55, November 1977, pp. 707-7 14, for further discussions of complexity issues.

[41] For more information, see CRS Report RL3 1775, *Do Budget Deficits Push Up Interest Rates and Is This the Relevant Question?*, by Marc Labonte.

[42] Although the credit crunch has increased the risk premium on borrowing rates and cut off access to credit for some risky borrowers, it has led to a general decline in interest rates.

[43] This relationship is due to the balance of payments accounting identity (i.e., dollars sold equals dollars bought).

[44] For more information, see CRS Report R40770, *Economic Effects of a Budget Deficit Exceeding $1 Trillion*, by Marc Labonte.

[45] U.S. Department of Treasury, *Troubled Asset Relief Program – Monthly Section 105(a) Report – November 2009*, December 10, 2009, available at *http://financialstability.gov/latest/reportsanddocs.html.*

[46] Congressional Budget Office, "Budget Savings from Legislated Reductions in Amounts Outstanding under the TARP," *Director's Blog*, December 10, 2009, *http://cboblog.cbo.gov/?p=440.*

[47] For example, CBO scored the $20.8 billion reduction in TARP authority in H.R. 4173 as a $10.4 billion reduction in the deficit in 2010. Congressional Budget Office, *Letter to Honorable Barney Frank*, December 9, 2009, *http://www.cbo.gov/ftpdocs/108xx/doc10844/hr4173asreported.pdf.* Since other provisions of this bill increased the deficit, the overall effect of the bill is to reduce the deficit by $7.3 billion over 10 years.

In: Unemployment: A Closer Look
Editors: Jacob S. Mlakar
ISBN: 978-1-61122-762-8

Chapter 3

UNEMPLOYMENT COMPENSATION (UC) AND THE UNEMPLOYMENT TRUST FUND (UTF): FUNDING UC BENEFITS

Julie M. Whittaker

SUMMARY

This report provides a summary of how Unemployment Compensation (UC) benefits are funded through the Unemployment Trust Fund (UTF). The UTF in the U.S. Treasury is designated as a trust fund for federal accounting purposes. Although the UTF is a single trust fund, it has 59 accounts: the Employment Security Administration Account (ESAA), the Extended Unemployment Compensation Account (EUCA), the Federal Unemployment Account (FUA), 53 state accounts, the Federal Employees Compensation Account (FECA), and two accounts related to the Railroad Retirement Board.

Federal unemployment taxes are credited to the ESAA; each state's unemployment taxes are credited to the state's unemployment account. Federal taxes pay for administration grants to the states. State unemployment taxes are dedicated to pay for regular UC benefits. The extended benefits (EB) program is typically funded 50% by the federal government and 50% by the states, but the 2009 stimulus package (The American Recovery and Reinvestment Act of 2009, P.L. 111- 5 § 2005, as amended) temporarily provides for 100% federal funding of EB through June 2, 2010. The stimulus package also includes a temporary supplemental unemployment benefit of $25 per week that is paid out of the general fund of the Treasury and not from the UTF.

This report will be updated as legislative activity warrants.

THE UNEMPLOYMENT COMPENSATION (UC) PROGRAM

Unemployment Compensation (UC) is a joint federal-state program financed by federal taxes under the Federal Unemployment Tax Act (FUTA) and by state payroll taxes under the State Unemployment Tax Acts (SUTA). The underlying framework of the UC system is contained in the Social Security Act (SSA). Title III of the SSA authorizes grants to states for the administration of state UC laws; Title IX authorizes the various components of the federal Unemployment Trust Fund (UTF); and Title XII authorizes advances or loans to insolvent state UC programs.

Federal Unemployment Tax Act

If a state UC program complies with all federal rules, the net FUTA tax rate for employers is 0.8% on the first $7,000 of each worker's earnings. The 0.8% FUTA tax funds both federal and state administrative costs as well as the federal share of the Extended Benefit (EB) program, loans to insolvent state UC accounts, and state employment services. Federal law defines which jobs a state UC program must cover for the state's employers to avoid paying the maximum FUTA tax rate (6.2%) on the first $7,000 of each employee's annual pay.

Expiring Provision: FUTA Surtax

On July 1, 2011, the effective FUTA tax on employers for each employee will decrease to 0.6% (down from 0.8%) on the first $7,000 of wages. P.L. 111-92, the Worker, Homeowner, and Business Assistance Act of 2009, extended the surtax for 1.5 years from December 2009 through June 2011.[1]

State Unemployment Tax Acts

States levy their own payroll taxes on employers to fund regular UC benefits and the state share of the EB program. The SUTA tax rate of an employer is, in most states, based on the amount of UC benefits paid to former employees. Generally, the more UC benefits paid to its former employees, the higher the tax rate of the employer, up to a maximum established by state law.

THE UNEMPLOYMENT TRUST FUND

The UTF is designated, by law, as a trust fund in the U.S. Treasury. The designation as a trust fund is a federal accounting mechanism to directly link revenues and distributions connected to the UC programs. The UTF accounts include the Employment Security Administration Account (ESAA), the Extended Unemployment Compensation Account (EUCA), the Federal Unemployment Account (FUA), 53 state accounts,[2] the Federal Employees Compensation Account (FECA), and two accounts related to the Railroad Retirement Board.[3] Federal unemployment taxes are credited to the ESAA; each state's unemployment taxes are credited to in the state's unemployment account. Federal taxes are dedicated to pay for UC administration grants to the states—including administration of extended benefits (EB) program—and the federal share of EB. State taxes are dedicated to pay for regular UC benefits and the state share of EB. Typically, the EB program is funded 50% by the federal government and 50% by the states, however, the 2009 stimulus package (P.L. 111-5 §2005, as amended) temporarily provides for 100% federal funding of EB through June 2, 2010.

The stimulus package also included a change in the financing structure of the emergency unemployment compensation program (EUC08); the EUC08 program is now paid by the general fund of the Treasury (previous to the enactment of the stimulus package, the benefits were paid out of the federal accounts within the UTF). The stimulus package also created a temporary supplemental benefit of $25 per week, which is paid by the general fund of the Treasury and not by the UTF.

Although the UTF contains 59 separate accounts (often referred to as *book accounts*) to attribute and distribute the monies appropriately based on program purpose, the UTF is a single trust fund. The use of separate accounts means that revenues and distributions are directly linked to UC program purpose. The use of a single trust fund (the UTF) for all UC programs permits a balance to carry over surplus spending authority to subsequent years. The balance represents reserve spending authority available in addition to the spending authority provided by the automatic appropriation of current tax receipts. This reserve spending authority is used during recessions when UC outlays exceed UTF tax revenues; that is, when current spending exceeds current receipts. Like many of the UTF 's other transactions, the balance is effectively a bookkeeping entry.

The Unemployment Trust Fund and the Federal Budget

All UC tax receipts and outlays for benefits and administration flow through the Treasury, and thus affect federal revenue, outlays, and the overall financial position (deficit or surplus) of the federal government. The UTF accounts for all UC financial transactions. This accounting device (designation as a trust fund) is used to accumulate legal spending authority that is available automatically when needed. However, the UTF does not contain financial resources. The required cash the federal government needs to pay benefits or administrative costs must be drawn from current resources through either taxation or borrowing. The revenue and the expenditures of the UC system are counted in the federal budget.

Federal laws require that excess UC funds be "invested" in federal government securities. However, because the UTF is a federal account, its holdings of federal securities are simply obligations from the federal government to itself. These obligations represent a budgetary resource to the UC program, not a financial resource to the federal government. This is because, while no cash has been raised, the interest earned on the investments is credited to the UTF. Because the federal government is holding its own securities, no cash is raised when these securities are liquidated. The UTF 's federal securities must be backed by cash raised through taxation or additional public borrowing. All things being equal, a UTF surplus reduces the federal deficit, lowering the amount the federal government must borrow from the public. Conversely, a UTF deficit increases the overall federal budget deficit and increases federal borrowing needs.

Unemployment Trust Fund Revenues and Distributions

The UTF is credited[4] with revenues from three primary sources:

- state unemployment taxes on employers,
- federal unemployment taxes on employers, and
- U.S. government agency transfers.

Although UC benefits are taxable and are fully subject to the federal income tax, those revenues do not support the UC system.[5] These three types of revenues are depicted at the top of **Figure 1**.

State Unemployment Tax Revenues Are Credited to the State Unemployment Accounts Within the Unemployment Trust Fund

States are authorized to designate that these funds be used to pay UC benefits. State unemployment account funds that are attributable to state unemployment taxes may only be used for unemployment benefits and the state's portion of extended unemployment benefits. Administrative costs are funded through distributions from the ESAA to the state unemployment accounts. At the end of FY2009, states were estimated to have collected $31.1 billion while expending $75.3 billion in regular UC benefits.

Federal Unemployment Taxes Are Credited to the ESAA

Each fiscal year, funds are appropriated through the federal budget process to make distributions from the ESAA for the states' costs of administering their unemployment compensation programs, and for the federal costs of administration. The Secretary of Labor determines (certifies) the amount of the administrative payments, and permits the Secretary of the Treasury to make the payments to the states. The Secretary of Labor in certifying a state for payment takes into account that (1) the state's UC programs contain specific provisions related to the payment of monies from the state unemployment system, (2) the state agency's specific responsibilities in administering the UC program and UC benefits, and (3) the rights and responsibilities of the UC benefit recipients.

Each Month, the ESAA Distributes 20% of the Net Monthly Activity to the EUCA

Net monthly activity is the sum of revenues credited to the ESAA less distributions for refunds of FUTA taxes and additional taxes attributable to a reduced credit for SUTA taxes. By the end of FY2009, the federal accounts had collected an estimated $6.66 billion; the ESAA held $0.21 billion. Since the ceiling for the ESAA was $2.08 billion, no excess funds were transferred to the EUCA. At the end of FY2009, the ESAA had distributions of $4.32 billion to the states for UC administrative costs.

If states have an active EB program, EUCA distributions are made for the federal portion (50% in permanent law; 100% as required by P.L. 111-5, as amended) of EB benefits. Prior to the passage of P.L. 111-5, the temporary Emergency Unemployment Compensation (EUC08) program funds were also are paid out of EUCA.[6] At the fiscal year end after any required distribution from the ESAA, the balance in the EUCA is determined. The EUCA balance is limited to the maximum of $750 million or 0.5% of covered wages.[7] If the EUCA balance exceeds the limitation, the excess is distributed to the FUA. At the end of FY2009 $4.12 billion was expended to pay for the federal share of EB benefits, and approximately $32.66 billion was expended on the EUC08 program. The EUCA balance was $0.58 billion. The EUCA ceiling was $24.12 billion; thus, there was no fund transfer to the FUA.

In addition to any EUCA distribution, the FUA is credited with the additional taxes paid by employers when a reduced credit against federal taxes exists because the state has an outstanding unpaid loan from FUA. FUA funds are distributed as loans to states, through the state unemployment accounts. (See the discussion below on “Loans to Insolvent Accounts” for a more detailed explanation of these loans.) The FUA balance is limited to the maximum of $550 million or 0.5% of covered wages. At the end of FY2008, the FUA balance was $4.42 billion; however, $6.8 billion had been loaned to the states, so the net balance was -$2.38 billion. This balance was lower than the $24.12 billion ceiling.

Distributions are made to the state unemployment accounts from the FECA to reimburse the states for employment compensation paid to former federal employees. Each federal agency reimburses the UTF for its share of federal workers’ UC benefits.

UTF Revenues

State Unemployment Taxes

Employers required to pay state unemployment taxes may remit their state unemployment taxes to states on a monthly, quarterly, annual, or another basis as determined by state laws and regulations. States, in turn, then remit the collected taxes to the Treasury. These funds are credited to the appropriate state unemployment account in the UTF.

Federal Unemployment Taxes

Employers may also be required to pay FUTA taxes on a quarterly basis. If the estimated quarterly federal tax is less than $500, an employer may roll the liability over to the next quarter until the liability is $500 or more. At that point, the employer must pay the FUTA taxes to the Treasury. An annual tax return reconciles the quarterly deposits to the actual tax liability. The ESAA is credited with the federal unemployment taxes.

U.S. Government Agency Transfers

Each federal agency is responsible for UC benefits paid on the agency's behalf. Each agency must budget for the unemployment benefits paid and reimburse the UTF for unemployment compensation paid on its behalf by states. The funds are credited to the FECA.

Other Unemployment Trust Fund Expenditures (Reed Act Distributions)

At the end of the fiscal year, there is a limitation on the balance in the ESAA—the account balance cannot exceed 40% of the prior fiscal year's appropriation by Congress. If the balance in the ESAA exceeds this limitation, the excess is distributed to EUCA. After the distribution, if the balance in the EUCA exceeds the limitation, the excess is distributed to the FUA. If after the distribution from the EUCA, the FUA balance exceeds the limitation, the excess is distributed, as a Reed Act distribution, to the states.[8] At the end of FY2009 there was no Reed Act distribution.

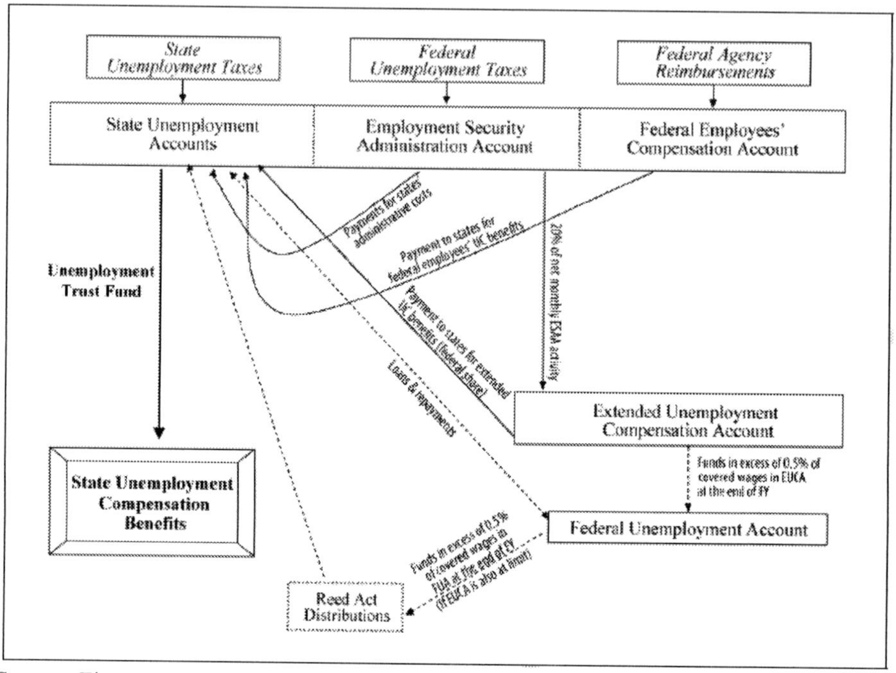

Source: Figures prepared by the Congressional Research Service (CRS).

Figure 1 . The Unemployment Trust Fund

Loans to Insolvent Accounts

The Treasury can write checks for a state unemployment account, provided that legal spending authority exists for such spending.[9] That is, the state unemployment account has a positive balance. During some recessions, current taxes and reserve balances were insufficient to cover expenditures for UC benefits. Some state unemployment accounts required "loans." Like all other transactions of the UTF, these are book account transactions that involve no exchange of cash. The loans are additional credits to a state unemployment account. Subsequent repayment of these loans reduces the credits in the state unemployment accounts.

The state unemployment accounts can borrow from the FUA. The principal of the loan is repaid by reducing federal tax credits for SUTA taxes and crediting those increased revenues to the FUA. The state cannot pay the interest on such loans using the state unemployment account but must pay the interest through state general revenues or other measures. Federal law also authorizes appropriations if balances in the federal accounts are insufficient to cover their expenditures. For example, if the states' borrowing needs exceed the available FUA balance, Congress is authorized to appropriate additional spending authority to cover the amount needed. Such appropriations require discretionary action by Congress and the President.

End Notes

[1] P.L. 94-566 first imposed the 0.2% surtax, increasing the net FUTA tax from 0.5% to 0.7% on the first $6,000 of earnings. The surtax was to be eliminated when all advances to the states had been repaid. P.L. 97-248 extended the surtax (increasing the net FUTA tax from 0.6% to 0.8%, on the first $7,000 of earnings) until the EUCA (Emergency Unemployment Compensation Account dedicated to funding the extended benefit program) loans were repaid. P.L. 100-203 extended the 0.2% surtax for three years—until January 1991. P.L. 10 1-508 extended the surtax for five years—until January 1996. P.L. 102-164 extended the surtax for an additional year—until January 1997. P.L. 103-66 extended the surtax for an additional two years—until January 2000. P.L. 105-34 extended the surtax for an additional nine years—until January 2008. P.L. 110-140 and P.L. 110-343 each extended the surtax for one additional year.

[2] The District of Columbia, Puerto Rico, and the Virgin Islands are considered to be states in UC matters.

[3] For the purposes of this report, the Railroad funds will be ignored.

[4] All revenues associated with UC are deposited to the U.S. Treasury, and all UC distributions (payments) are made by the U.S. Treasury. The revenues and distributions made by the U.S. Treasury are linked to the different UC programs and purposes through the federal accounting mechanism of the UTF and its separate accounts.

[5] This differs from funds from the taxation of Social Security benefits that help support the Social Security and Medicare programs.

[6] With the passage of P.L. 111-5, the EUC08 program is now 100% financed by the federal government through general funds within the U.S. Treasury.

[7] P.L. 105-33 increased the statutory ceiling on the FUA from 0.25% to 0.5% of covered wages, effective October 1, 2001. P.L. 102-318, had lowered the FUA from 0.625% to 0.25% and increased the ceiling for EUCA from 0.375% to 0.5%. P.L. 100-203, had raised the EUCA ceiling from 0.125% to .375% and increased the FUA ceiling from 0.125% to 0.625%.

[8] For more information on Reed Act distributions, see CRS Report RS22006, *The Unemployment Trust Fund and Reed Act Distributions*, by Julie M. Whittaker.

[9] For details on loans to insolvent accounts, see CRS Report RS22954, *The Unemployment Trust Fund (UTF): State Insolvency and Federal Loans to States*, by Julie M. Whittaker.

In: Unemployment: A Closer Look
Editors: Jacob S. Mlakar
ISBN: 978-1-61122-762-8

Chapter 4

UNEMPLOYMENT COMPENSATION (INSURANCE) AND MILITARY SERVICE

Julie M. Whittaker

SUMMARY

The Unemployment Compensation (UC) program contains several provisions relevant to current and former military service personnel and their families. The UC program does not provide benefits for military servicemembers on active duty. However, former active duty military personnel (and certain reservists) separated from active duty may be eligible for Unemployment Compensation for Ex-Servicemembers (UCX).

Spouses of military service personnel who voluntarily quit a job to accompany their spouses on account of a military transfer may be eligible for UC benefits, based on the laws of the state where the civilian spouse was employed.

Military service of business owners, employees, and employees' spouses may impact the state unemployment tax rate that certain employers face. States may choose to create provisions that remove or limit these tax increases in certain situations.

Individuals should contact their state's unemployment agency to obtain information on how to apply for and receive unemployment benefits based upon military service. The U.S. Department of Labor maintains a website with links to each state's agency at *http://www.workforcesecurity.doleta.gov/map.asp*.

This report will be updated as events warrant.

Unemployment Compensation Benefit Eligibility for Former Military Personnel

Unemployment Compensation for Ex-Servicemembers (UCX)[1] provides income support while former active duty military personnel or reservists[2] released from active duty search for work. The Emergency Unemployment Compensation Act of 1991 (P.L. 102-164) provides that exservicemembers be treated the same as other unemployed workers with respect to benefit levels, the waiting period for benefits, and benefit duration.[3]

Once entitlement to regular unemployment benefits are exhausted, ex-servicemembers may qualify for both Emergency Unemployment Compensation (EUC08) and the Extended Benefit (EB) payments.[4] All benefits (UCX, EUC08, and EB) are temporarily augmented by the weekly $25 Federal Additional Compensation (FAC) payment.

The federal government funds these benefits through the transfers from the appropriate military services' budgets[5] to the Unemployment Trust Fund[6] (UTF) to reimburse the appropriate states for the UCX benefits distributed to unemployed ex-servicemembers. For the 12 month period ending March 2010, approximately $1,185 million in unemployment benefits (UCX, EUC08, EB, and the $25 FAC) were distributed to former military personnel.

Military personnel on active duty do not qualify for regular state Unemployment Compensation (UC) or UCX benefits because they are considered to be working.

UCX Eligibility and Benefit Level

Ex-servicemembers generally apply for UCX benefits in the state where they are searching for employment. UC eligibility criteria and benefits vary by state. The ex-servicemembers must meet the same criteria that civilian workers are required to meet for their UC benefit eligibility. Thus, two ex-servicemembers with the same earnings and work history may qualify for different amounts of benefits if they file for UCX in different states. The equivalent military measurement of wages and time in service are used to determine eligibility and benefit levels.[7]

If the ex-servicemember was originally in the active duty military, he or she must have left military service under honorable conditions and either completed a full term of service or have been released early under a qualifying reason. If the ex-servicemember was a reservist formerly on active duty, he or she must have been on active duty for at least 90 continuous days. UCX benefits are not payable during periods in which the ex-servicemember is eligible to receive certain allowances or educational assistance allowances from the Survivors' and Dependents' Educational Assistance Program or the Department of Veterans' Affairs Vocational Rehabilitation and Education Program. Participation in the Montgomery GI bill does not preclude receipt of UCX benefits; however, having student status does limit UC benefit eligibility in most states and these limitations would extend to those workers receiving UCX benefits. Many states exclude workers while they attend school and some states include vacation periods in that exclusion.

Self-Employed and Sole Proprietor Ex-Servicemembers

When an ex-servicemember was previously self-employed or was a sole-proprietor, the worker would have been excluded from receiving UC benefits. After active duty, if the ex-servicemember is unemployed, the ex-servicemember would qualify for UCX benefits based on military service. However, most states require that the worker be searching for employment and would not cover a worker who was reestablishing self-employment or a small business.[8]

UCX Financing

The UCX benefit is funded by the federal government through its federal account in the Unemployment Trust Fund (UTF)[9]. Each state is reimbursed by the federal government for each unemployed worker whose base period wages included federal military wages.

Civilian Spouses Who Quit Employment Because of Military Spouse Transfers

Civilian spouses who quit their employment because their military spouse was transferred may not qualify for UC benefits. Many state UC programs do not award UC benefits to workers who quit their jobs because a spouse was transferred, deeming this as a "voluntary quit." The laws of three states (Maryland, Ohio, and Texas) go further and include a specific disqualification for claimants who quit work to relocate with a spouse until certain additional income is generated. However, Maryland and Texas both exempt military spouses from this disqualification.

The disqualification following a "voluntary quit" continues until the claimant returns to work, completes a specified duration of work, and earns wages of a specified amount. In other states, the disqualification is time-limited. These states penalize the worker for quitting, but recognize that economic conditions may be such that even a person who diligently seeks work may find none. The reasoning is that beyond a certain point, if a diligent job seeker is still unemployed, such continuing unemployment is attributable to labor market conditions rather than their decision to quit. Thus, spouses relocating to areas of high unemployment or limited opportunities may become eligible for benefits even if initially disqualified.

Transferred Spouse Exception (Unconditional on Military Service)

Twenty-three states allow workers who quit because of their spouse's job transfer to receive UC benefits. **Table 1** lists these states, designating them in the column labeled "Spouse Transfer" with a "Y."

Military Spouse Exception

In addition to the 23 states allowing UC benefits if a worker quits to accompany a spouse who has been transferred, 15 states have special exceptions for workers who quit to join their transferred military spouse. These exceptions are labeled as "Military only" or "Federal spouse" in **Table**

1. Thus, a total of 38 states allow the civilian spouse of a transferred military servicemember to receive UC benefits.

Table 1. Unemployment Compensation Benefit Eligibility for Workers Who Voluntarily Quit Because of a Spousal Transfer

State	Spouse Transfer	State	Spouse Transfer
Alabama		Montana	Military only
Alaska	Y	Nebraska	Y
Arizona	Y	Nevada	Y
Arkansas	Y	New Hampshire	Y
California	Y	New Jersey	Military only
Colorado	Y	New Mexico	Military only
Connecticut	Y	New York	Y
Delaware	Y	North Carolina	Y
District of Columbia	Military only	North Dakota	
Florida	Military only	Ohio	
Georgia	Military only	Oklahoma	Y
Hawaii	Y	Oregon	Y
Idaho		Pennsylvania	Y
Illinois	Y	Rhode Island	
Indiana	Y	South Carolina	Military only
Iowa		South Dakota	
Kansas	Y	Tennessee	
Kentucky	Military only	Texas	Military only
Louisiana		Utah	
Maine	Y	Vermont	
Maryland	Military only	Virginia	Military only
Massachusetts	Y	Washington	Y
Michigan	Military only	West Virginia	
Minnesota	Y	Wisconsin	
Mississippi	Military only	Wyoming	Military only
Missouri	Federal spouse only		

Source: CRS compilation from *Comparison of State Unemployment Insurance Laws, 2010 (and errata)*, and interim updates, U.S. Department of Labor, Employment and Training Administration, Office of Workforce Security. Additional requirements may be imposed to qualify for these exceptions.

Impact of Military Service on Employers' State Unemployment Taxes

State unemployment taxes are levied on employers based on a combination of established rates and the employer's past history of its workers using the UC system. Generally, employers with a greater history of unemployed workers would have a worse experience rating and would pay higher state unemployment taxes. Military service of business owners or employees may impact the tax rate that certain employers face. Furthermore, if workers who quit to join a transferred military spouse receive UC benefits, this may impact the overall state unemployment tax burden of most, if not all, of the state's employers. Below are some examples of these situations.

- A business owner, if called up for active military service, may need to lay off some or all of the business's workers. Once the business owner returns from military service, the revival of the business may mean that the small business may face a new, higher state unemployment tax rate.
- If the servicemember serves for less than two years, some of the worker's UCX benefit may be based on nonmilitary work. (These workers receive a hybrid UC/UCX benefit.) In some states, their former (civilian) employers may face a state unemployment tax increase as a result.
- Workers who quit their jobs and move to accompany their military spouse may receive UC benefits in 38 states. These states do not charge UC benefits to employer accounts when workers voluntarily quit their jobs to accompany a transferred military spouse. The benefits paid to a worker accompanying a military spouse generally would not increase the state unemployment taxes of the worker's former employer. However, these benefits are still charged to the state's account within the UTF. As a result, the cost of the benefits are passed on to the state's employers as a socialized cost and may increase the overall state unemployment tax rate.

States may choose to create provisions that remove or limit these tax increases in certain situations. For example:

- In Illinois, business owners who are called to active duty from the reserve and had to close their firms are not charged for the increases attributable to UC benefits for the workers who lose their jobs on account of the closure. When the business owner returns and reopens his or her business, the business's state unemployment tax rate is not increased.
- In Texas, if an employee was called to active military service but then qualifies for UC benefits, the employer does not face a higher state unemployment tax rate.
- Maine, South Dakota, Montana, Virginia, Washington, and Wyoming provide for the non-charging of benefits for unemployment directly resulting from reinstatement of another employee upon his or her completion of uniformed service duty.

End Notes

[1] Established by the Ex-servicemen's Unemployment Act of 1958 (P.L. 85-848, 5 U.S.C. §§ 8521-8525) in 1958.

[2] In this report, the terms *reserves* or *reservists* include the Army and Air National Guard and their servicemembers.

[3] Previously, in 1982, Congress had placed restrictions on benefits for ex-servicemembers (P.L. 97-3 62). In addition to a number of restrictive eligibility requirements, ex-servicemembers were required to wait four weeks from the date of their separation from the service before they could receive benefits. The maximum number of weeks of benefits an ex-servicemember could receive based on employment in the military was 13 (as compared with 26 weeks under the regular UC program for civilian workers).

[4] For information on the EUC08 benefit, see CRS Report RS22915, *Temporary Extension of Unemployment Benefits: Emergency Unemployment Compensation (EUC08)*, by Katelin P. Isaacs, Julie M. Whittaker, and Alison M. Shelton. For information on the Extended Benefit program, see CRS Report RL33362, *Unemployment Insurance: Available Unemployment Benefits and Legislative Activity*, by Julie M. Whittaker, Alison M. Shelton, and Katelin P. Isaacs.

[5] For example, if a former naval officer claimed UCX benefits, the Navy would transfer funds into the UTF to pay for those benefits.

[6] For details on the Unemployment Trust Fund, see CRS Report RS22077, *Unemployment Compensation (UC) and the Unemployment Trust Fund (UTF): Funding UC Benefits*, by Julie M. Whittaker and Kathleen Romig.

[7] The state in which the former servicemember files for a claim determines the UCX benefit level and duration. The weekly and maximum amounts of UCX payable to an individual under the UCX program are determined under the applicable state laws. The UCX benefit is required to be the same amount, on the same terms, and subject to the same conditions as the state UC that would be payable to the individual under the applicable state law. The individual's federal military service and federal military wages are assigned or transferred as employment and wages covered by that state law, subject to the use of the applicable Schedule of Remuneration. That is, for claims purposes, military wages are determined by

the pay grade at separation from military service. A wage table is provided by the federal government to calculate the equivalent civilian wages for each military pay grade.

[8] An exception to this are those states that offer a Self-Employment Assistance (SEA) program. Eight states have active SEA programs: Delaware, Maine, Maryland, New Jersey, New York, Oregon, Pennsylvania, and Washington. Individuals enrolled in an SEA program receive weekly allowances. These allowances are the same as the individual's regular unemployment weekly benefit amount. Participants engaged full-time in activities relating to the establishment of a business and becoming self-employed are considered to be unemployed. Provisions of state law relating to availability for work, search for work, and refusal to accept work do not apply to these participants.

[9] See CRS Report RS22077, *Unemployment Compensation (UC) and the Unemployment Trust Fund (UTF): Funding UC Benefits*, by Julie M. Whittaker and Kathleen Romig, for an explanation of how funds are transferred.

In: Unemployment: A Closer Look
Editors: Jacob S. Mlakar
ISBN: 978-1-61122-762-8

Chapter 5

DOES UNEMPLOYMENT INSURANCE INHIBIT JOB SEARCH?

Carolyn Maloney

The Unemployment Compensation (UC) program contains several provisions relevant to current and former military service personnel and their families. The UC program does not provide benefits for military servicemembers on active duty. However, former active duty military personnel (and certain reservists) separated from active duty may be eligible for Unemployment Compensation for Ex-Servicemembers (UCX).

Spouses of military service personnel who voluntarily quit a job to accompany their spouses on account of a military transfer may be eligible for UC benefits, based on the laws of the state where the civilian spouse was employed.

Unemployment benefits are not particularly generous – average weekly benefits are just 74 percent of the poverty threshold for a family of four.[1] So it is unlikely that extended unemployment benefits inhibit individuals' job search efforts. Simply put, even a low-paying job is likely to provide more support than that offered by UI. Moreover, five unemployed Americans exist for every job opening today, which means that individuals who exhaust benefits are unlikely to find a new job with ease. Those who remain jobless and without unemployment benefits will need some form of social assistance in order to avoid complete destitution, and are likely to turn to alternative social programs at a cost to the federal government.

Extending unemployment insurance benefits is not only a critical form of economic security for American families, but also a key form of fiscal stimulus that has the potential to ease pressure on the labor market by stimulating economic growth.

UNEMPLOYMENT INSURANCE DOES NOT DISCOURAGE JOB SEARCH BEHAVIOR

While earlier research suggested that the unemployment insurance program in the 1970s and 1980s had important disincentive effects, the current consensus is that these dated studies overstated the effects of unemployment insurance benefits on job search behavior. The older studies noted a jump in the fraction of workers who found a job just before they exhausted their benefits.[2] In contrast, in testimony before the Joint Economic Committee, the author of one of the seminal papers in this earlier wave of research, Dr. Lawrence Katz, said that "the most compelling research shows only modest impacts of UI extensions on the search effort and duration of unemployment of unemployment insurance recipients."[3] For example, Katz argued that the large effects found in these earlier studies were mainly due to "firms and industries using temporary layoffs and the sensitivity of recall dates to unemployment insurance benefits," and suggested that the "layoff-recall process is much less important today than it was in the 1970s and early 1980s."[4] Katz pointed out that these studies overstate the overall impact of unemployment insurance benefits on the length of unemployment spells "by ignoring the spillover effects of shorter unemployment spells for the other unemployed workers not receiving UI benefits."[5]

Dr. Katz is not the only economist who holds these views. Dr. Till von Wachter, in testimony before the Joint Economic Committee, also shared Katz's opinion.[6] "It is likely that in severe recessions, the benefit of extended UI outweighs the costs," argues von Wachter.[7] Analyzing data from Germany that was of much higher quality than most other studies on the disincentive effects of unemployment insurance, von Wachter found that "extended UI would lead to a moderate increase in the rate of unemployment." He also inferred that the increase in the unemployment rate would be smaller in the United States right now because labor market conditions are tight and jobs are scarce.[8]

Another prominent economist who has studied unemployment insurance and other social insurance programs, Dr. Raj Chetty, has reached similar conclusions. In one paper, he and co- authors showed that even though there is a "spike" in exit rates from unemployment insurance at the time of benefit exhaustion, the probability of reemployment doesn't change significantly.[9] In other words, many of those who exit the unemployment insurance rolls as their benefits are about to expire are not moving on to another job. Furthermore, Chetty argues that "work disincentive effects" are likely to be small because people are "likely to take any job they can get" in the current economic downturn.[10]

Former Chairman of the Federal Reserve Alan Greenspan has also expressed strong support for extending unemployment insurance benefits, and dismisses the argument that unemployment benefits discourage job search behavior. In testimony to the Joint Economic Committee, Chairman Greenspan said, "[U]nemployment benefit insurance here is essentially restrictive because it's been our perception that we don't want to create incentives for people not to take jobs. But when you're in period of job weakness where it is not a choice on the part of people whether or not they're employed or unemployed, then, obviously, you want to be temporarily generous. And that's what we've done in the past, and I think it's worked well."[11]

While an extension of unemployment insurance benefits will not discourage job search behavior, it may increase the reported unemployment rate by a small amount. This is because the unemployment rate counts only those individuals who are actively seeking work, which is a requirement for receiving unemployment insurance benefits. Jobless individuals who drop out of the labor market entirely are not counted when the Bureau of Labor Statistics calculates the unemployment rate. Because unemployment insurance incentivizes labor force attachment, an extension of these benefits means that more jobless Americans will be counted as unemployed.

THE CURRENT LABOR MARKET PROVIDES FEW OPPORTUNITIES FOR UNEMPLOYED WORKERS

There are currently 5 unemployed workers for every job opening.[12] The slack labor market means that an unemployed worker who loses benefits faces a serious challenge in securing new employment. The jobs are simply not there yet.

In the absence of unemployment benefits, job seekers need some form of assistance in order to avoid further economic crisis. Private savings are not the answer, as the vast majority of unemployed Americans have minimal savings on which to draw upon during jobless spells. Indeed, economist Raj Chetty finds that nearly half of job losers in the United States report zero liquid wealth at the time of job loss, suggesting that many households simply do not have the resources to continue to pay their bills and put food on the table in the absence of unemployment insurance benefits.[13]

In the absence of unemployment insurance benefits or private savings, these workers will need an alternative source of income until they find employment. In the wake of the financial crisis, banks have tightened lending requirements, which constrains access to credit cards and home equity lines for economically-vulnerable Americans.[14] Many are likely to turn to another social assistance program that may be even more expensive than unemployment insurance. For instance, the Joint Economic Committee estimates that the cost of failure to extend unemployment benefits would result in $24.2 billion in additional spending on Disability Insurance benefits.[15] Other programs, including Temporary Assistance to Needy Families and food stamps (now SNAP), are likely to see a spike as well.

Unemployment Insurance as Effective Fiscal Stimulus

Workers receiving unemployment insurance payments are typically cash-strapped and will spend their benefits quickly. This quick spending generates a "multiplier" for the economy as a whole. Every dollar of unemployment benefits that a recipient spends can generate a cascade of spending by others, providing a significant jolt to the nation's economy in terms of both economic activity and employment. Therefore, extending unemployment insurance benefits not only helps struggling households, but can also spur the creation of job opportunities.

Indeed, the President's Council of Economic Advisers estimates that every dollar spent on unemployment insurance benefits raises gross domestic product (GDP) by $1.60.[16] The nonpartisan Congressional Budget Office recently reported that increasing aid to the unemployed is more cost-effective in terms of boosting economic growth and employment than a variety of other policies under consideration.[17] Given forecasts of tepid growth through the rest of 2010 and 2011, additional targeted stimulus should be discussed in Congress.

End Notes

[1] Joint Economic Committee calculations using data from the Congressional Research Service and the Department of Health and Human Services. See Whittaker, Julie, et. al. May 28, 1010. "Unemployment Insurance: Unemployment Benefits and Legislative Activity." http://crs.gov/Pages/Reports.aspx?Source=search&ProdCode=RL33362; United States Department of Health and Human Services Assistant Secretary for Planning and Evaluation, 2009 Federal Poverty Guidelines, http://aspe.hhs.gov/poverty

[2] Katz, Lawrence F. and Bruce D. Meyer. "The Impact of the Potential Duration of Unemployment Benefits on the Duration of Unemployment," *Journal of Public Economics* (1990), pp. 45-72.

[3] Joint Economic Committee testimony of Dr. Lawrence Katz (April 29, 2010).

[4] *Ibid.*

[5] *Ibid.*

[6] Joint Economic Committee testimony of Dr. Till von Wachter (April 29, 2010).

[7] *Ibid.* In testimony before the House Committee on Ways and Means, "Responding to Long-Term Unemployment," June 10, 2010, Dr. von Wachter further testified that "As a typical measure, extensions of unemployment insurance have been shown to prevent large consumption declines of laid off workers; thereby, they provide a degree of demand stabilization; they are also likely to prevent entry into more costly government programs such as disability insurance; and – at least in recessions – extensions of the duration of unemployment insurance benefits are unlikely to be associated with significant reductions in employment in the short or the long run."

[8] *Ibid.*

[9] Card, David, Raj Chetty, and Andrea Weber. "The Spike at Benefit Exhaustion: Leaving the Unemployment System or Starting a New Job?" August 2007 NBER working paper.

[10] From Dr. Raj Chetty's May 28, 2010 presentation before the Economic Policy Institute on "Should Unemployment Benefits Be Extended: An Economic Framework and Empirical Evidence." His presentation can be found at http://epi.3cdn.net/d5a99f04921083739f t7m6bxpa7.pdf.

[11] Testimony of the Honorable Alan Greenspan, Chairman, Board of Governors of the Federal Reserve System, Joint Economic Committee (May 21, 2003).

[12] Joint Economic Committee calculation using data from the Bureau of Labor Statistics Job Openings and Labor Turnover Survey and the Bureau of Labor Statistics Household Survey.

[13] Chetty, Raj. Moral Hazard vs. Liquidity and Optimal Unemployment Insurance. http://www.econ.berkeley.edu/~chetty/papers/mh liq ui jpe. pdf.

[14] Board of Governors of the Federal Reserve System. May 3, 2010. "The April 2010 Senior Loan Officer Opinion Survey on Bank Lending Practices." *http://www.federalreserve.gov/ boarddocs/SnLoanSurvey/201005/fullreport.pdf*

[15] Joint Economic Committee. May 2010. Extending Unemployment Insurance Benefits: The Cost of Inaction for Disabled Workers. *http://jec.senate.gov/public/?a=Files.Serve&Fileid=d5003466-eb78-4a91-b5b1-eb99c2982166.*

[16] Statement of Jane Oates, Assistant Secretary for Employment and Training, U.S. Department of Labor, Senate Finance Committee (April 14, 2010).

[17] Congressional Budget Office, Policies for Increasing Economic Growth and Employment in 2010 and 2011. January 2010. http://www.cbo.gov/ftpdocs/108xx/doc10803/01-14-Employment.pdf.

In: Unemployment: A Closer Look
Editors: Jacob S. Mlakar
ISBN: 978-1-61122-762-8

Chapter 6

UNDERSTANDING THE ECONOMY: WORKING MOTHERS IN THE GREAT RECESSION

Carolyn Maloney

MOTHER'S DAY 2010: AN UPDATE ON WORKING MOMS

The Great Recession has taken a huge toll on working families. The vast majority of jobs lost were lost by men, but a substantial number of jobs were lost by women during this recession. From December 2007 to April 2010, women lost 46 jobs for every 100 jobs lost by men.[1] By comparison, during the 2001 recession, women lost 17 jobs for every 100 lost by men and women lost less than 2 jobs for every 100 jobs lost by men during the 1990s recession. Indeed, in recent months, women lost jobs while men gained jobs.[2] From October 2009 to March 2010, women lost 22,000 jobs while men gained 260,000.[3] Women's increased vulnerability to the business cycle has important repercussions for families' economic security. This report provides an updated look at the employment situation of working mothers[4] with children under 18 years old, and examines the impact of the recession on their participation in the labor market using unpublished data from the Bureau of Labor Statistics.[5]

Families Depend on Mothers' Employment

Over the past several decades, women have played a role of growing importance in the labor force. It is clear that in the wake of the Great Recession, families continue to rely upon mothers' employment. Rather than opting out of the labor force, mothers increased their labor force participation over the recession. The share of mothers working or actively searching for work increased from 71.0 percent to 71.4 percent between 2007 and 2009.[6]

During that time, mothers' participation shifted away from full-time work to unemployment and part-time work, with the share of all mothers working full-time dropping to 48.3 percent in 2009 from 51.3 percent in 2007. (See Figure 1) The share of all mothers working part-time rose almost a full percentage point to 17.2 percent, while the share of unemployed mothers increased 2.6 percentage points to 5.9 percent.

Of the 21.7 million mothers who were usually employed in 2009, two-thirds were in a dual- earner family. But the remaining one-third—7.5 million mothers—were the sole job-holders in their family, either because their spouse was unemployed or out of the labor force, or because they were heads of household. (See Figure 2)

Figure 1. Nearly Half of All Mothers Worked Full Time Last Year

Employment Status of Women with Children Under 18 Years Old, 2009 Annual Averages

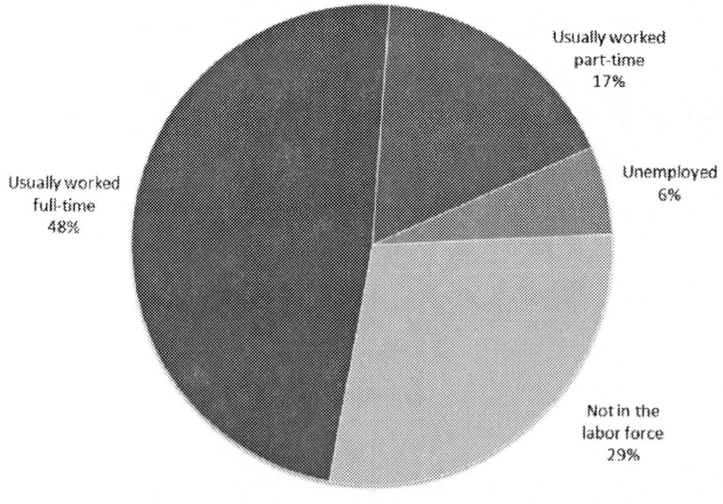

Source: Joint Economic Committee Majority Staff calculations based on unpublished data from the Bureau of Labor Statistics, Current Population Survey.

Figure 2. One-in-Three Working Mothers Was the Only Jobholder in Her Family

Employed Women in the Labor Force with Children Under 18 Years Old, 2009 Annual Averages

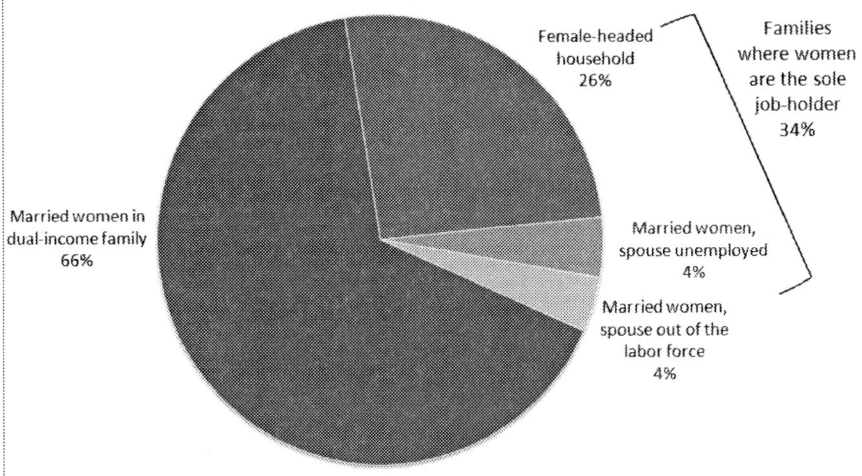

Source: Joint Economic Committee Majority Staff calculations based on unpublished data from the Bureau of Labor Statistics, Current Population Survey.

Married Mothers Search for Work to Improve Their Families' Economic Security

Until recently, job losses were concentrated in male-dominated industries like construction and manufacturing, so fathers were more likely to lose a job and mothers were more likely to hold onto their employment or quickly find a new job. As job losses slowed in the final months of 2009, women continued to lose jobs as men found employment.

In order to cope with the widespread job losses during the recession, many parents who were previously out of the labor force entered the workforce, presumably to compensate for a spouse's lost wages. In general, mothers are far more likely than fathers to be out of the labor force, thus the movement of parents into the labor market largely reflects that of mothers. In 2007, 35.2 percent of two-parent families had only one employed parent, compared to 36.8 percent in 2009. That 1.6 percentage point net difference masks more dramatic changes in the share of families solely dependent on a *mother's* earnings. In fact, families where the mother was the only jobholder rose 2.5

percentage points from 4.9 percent of married-couple families to 7.4 percent. More than ever, families depend on mothers' work.

Many married mothers who looked for employment in order to bolster their families' economic security found it difficult to find work because of the severe shortage of jobs. The labor force participation rate rose for married mothers between 2007 and 2009, meaning that more married mothers were searching for a job. However, the employment-to-population ratio—the so called 'employment rate'—fell over the recession from 66.7 percent to 65.5 percent, indicating that fewer married mothers actually had a job. The unemployment rate nearly doubled to 5.8 percent during that time—a clear sign that mothers wanting work struggled to find a job.

SINGLE MOTHERS CONTINUE TO STRUGGLE WITH HIGH UNEMPLOYMENT

Families headed by single mothers had no second parent to fall back on in the face of job loss or reduced hours and earnings. Labor force participation was already higher among these women, with over three-quarters (76.5 percent) of women maintaining families working or actively searching for work in 2007. Consequently, the recession did not boost their participation rate. Instead, the participation rate of mothers maintaining families dropped to 75.8 percent indicating that many single mothers dropped out of the labor force probably because they were unable to find work.

For single mothers in the labor force, unemployment increased dramatically during the recession. Between 2007 and 2009, the unemployment rate of single mothers increased from 8.0 percent to 13.6 percent. Single mothers of children under the age of 6 who are not yet in school had an unemployment rate of 17.5 percent in 2009. For these mothers, even searching for work can be a challenge because they may have to find child care in order to go on an interview, and high costs of child care eat away a substantial chunk of their earnings once they do find a job.

THE PART-TIME PENALTY CAN BE EVEN GREATER FOR MOTHERS

Many women have been unable to find full-time employment because of the weak labor market. In 2009, 3.3 million women worked part-time for economic reasons, meaning that either their hours had been cut back or that they searched for full-time work but could only a part-time job. Some of those part-time workers usually worked part-time but would have preferred to move to full-time work, likely because of economic hardship such as a spouse's job loss.

Part-time workers face a severe earnings penalty, with a wage equal to as little as 60 percent of the wage for full-time workers in the same occupation. (See Figure 3) Part-time work also means lower earnings over time, and part-time jobs usually do not come with the same health benefits, paid time-off for vacation and sick leave, or pension benefits that full-time workers receive.[7]

Over one-third (35 percent, or 6.2 million) of all women working part-time in 2009 were mothers. For many of those, including 2.7 million mothers with children less than 6 years old and not yet in school, working a part-time job also means finding part-time child care. The part- time earnings penalty is even more devastating for those mothers because part-time child care can be just as costly as full-time care.[8]

Figure 3. Part-Time Workers Are Subject to a Wage Penalty

Part-Time Wage as a Percent of Full-Time Wage by Occupation Broken Down

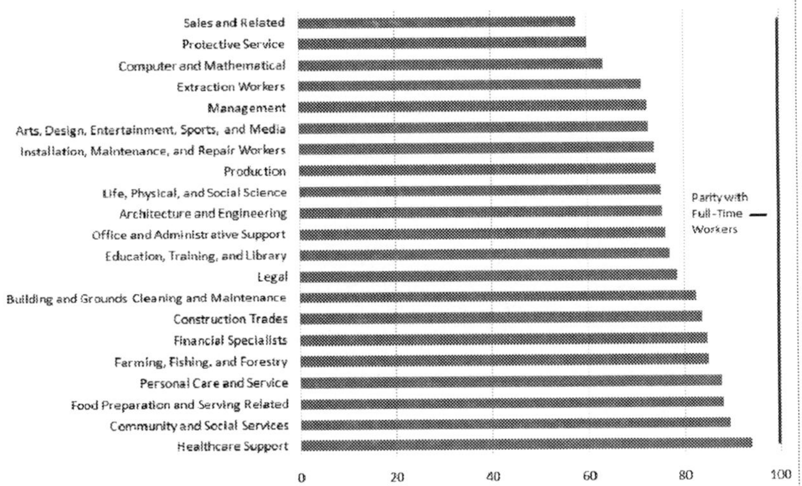

Source: Joint Economic Committee Majority Staff calculations based on data from the United States Census Bureau.

CONCLUSION

Families depend on women's earnings. Mothers' work is vital not only for their families' economic security, but also for the strength of the American economy as a whole. Understanding and addressing the impact of the Great Recession on mothers is a crucial piece of the economic recovery.

End Notes

1 Bureau of Labor Statistics, Current Employment Survey.

2 *Ibid.*

3 April's strong employment growth showed women gained 86,000 jobs last month, far fewer than the 204,000 jobs gained by men in April. Bureau of Labor Statistics, Current Employment Survey, April 2010.

4 The Joint Economic Committee released a report on working mothers last year. See *Women in the Recession: Working Mothers Face High Rates of Unemployment*, May 28, 2009.

5 Data is from Tables 4, 4a, and 6 using data from the Current Population Survey.

6 Unless otherwise specified, mother refers to a woman with her own children under the age of 18. Married mothers are those with a spouse who is present. Single mothers include married mothers with an absent spouse; divorced, separated, and widowed mothers; and mothers who have never been married.

7 See Joint Economic Committee report: *The Earnings Penalty for Part-Time Work*, April 20, 2010.

8 Many child care centers do not offer prorated part-time child care meaning that the per-hour cost for part-time care is higher than for full-time care.

In: Unemployment: A Closer Look
Editors: Jacob S. Mlakar
ISBN: 978-1-61122-762-8

Chapter 7

WOMEN IN THE RECESSION: WORKING MOTHERS FACE HIGH RATES OF UNEMPLOYMENT

Carolyn B. Maloney and Charles E. Schumer

EXECUTIVE SUMMARY

Working women have received pink slips in growing numbers over the course of the current recession, which began in December 2007. For the first 3 months of the recession, when job losses were relatively light, women actually gained rather than lost jobs. This uptick in women's employment is similar to what has happened in previous recessions. However, in August 2008, this recession began to look quite different from past downturns. Women's job losses picked up pace to become a significant fraction of the total monthly job losses.

As women's job losses have accelerated, so have the job losses for working mothers. A Joint Economic Committee analysis of published and unpublished data collected by the Bureau of Labor Statistics (BLS) finds that increases in unemployment during this recession have been especially steep for female heads of household – mothers who are solely responsible for maintaining their families' economic security. Key findings of the analysis include the following:

- In 2008, seven out of ten mothers with children under 18 years old were in the labor force. Over half of all mothers usually worked full time last year.
- As of April 2009, nearly one million working-age female heads of household wanted a job but could not find one.
- One out of every ten women maintaining a family is unemployed, which exceeds the highest rate (9.0 percent) experienced during the 2001 recession and the "jobless recovery" that followed.
- The ranks of female heads of household who are unemployed or "marginally attached" to the labor force has grown across all demographic groups, with women of color faring the worst. Black and Hispanic women in this group are currently experiencing unemployment at rates of 13.3 percent and 11.0 percent, respectively.

The American Recovery and Reinvestment Act (ARRA) will temper the effects of the current recession for these families right now and over time. Extended unemployment benefits, nutrition assistance programs, preserving Medicaid benefits and tax cuts will bring immediate relief for these families. In addition, ARRA invests in job creation in education, healthcare, and child care that tend to disproportionately employ women. This will help to ensure that female- headed households will not be left behind in the recovery.

Vast Majority of Mothers in the Labor Force, Most Work Full-Time

Women's increased vulnerability to the business cycle has significant implications for family economic well-being.[1] Most children grow up in families with working parents, regardless of whether they live in dual- or single-parent families. Today, many families no longer have an additional worker to enter the labor force when times are tough, making rising unemployment among women a worrisome trend.

On average, in 2008, seven out of ten (71.4 percent) mothers with children under 18 years old were in the labor force.[2] The remaining 29 percent were not in the labor force and were usually not counted in official unemployment statistics. Over half of all mothers worked full time during 2008. An additional 16 percent worked part time, while 4 percent of all mothers were unemployed. (See Figure 1) Of those employed mothers, about one-third were the sole breadwinners for the families – either because they were the head of the household or, for married women, because their spouses were unemployed or out of the labor force. (See Figure 2) Among those in the labor force, the unemployment rate for mothers with children under 18 years old averaged 5.6 percent in 2008, a full percentage point higher than in 2007.

As Recession Continues, Working Mothers Face Rising Unemployment

Working women have received pink slips in growing numbers over the course of the current recession. For the first 3 months of the recession, when job losses were relatively light, unlike men, women actually gained jobs.[3] This uptick in women's employment is similar to what has happened in previous recessions. However, in August 2008, this recession began to look quite different from past downturns as women's job losses picked up pace to become a significant fraction of the total monthly job losses. On average, one-third of jobs lost were held by women during the past eight months.

Figure 1. Over Half of All Mothers Worked Full Time Last Year
Employment Status of Women with Children Under 18 Years Old, 2008 Annual Averages

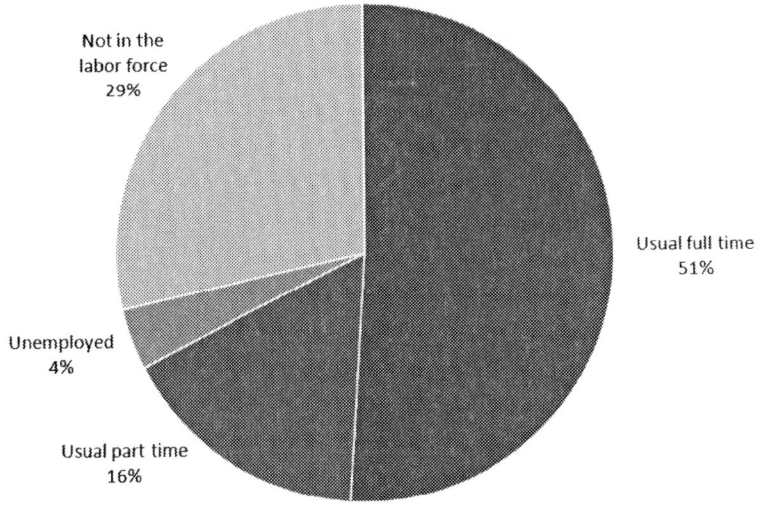

Source: JEC calculations based on data from Bureau of Labor Statistics, Current Population Survey.

Increases in unemployment during this recession have been especially steep for female heads of household, who are solely responsible for maintaining their families' economic security.[4] Among female heads of household, the unemployment rate rose 3.1 percentage points between December 2007 and April 2009, compared to an increase of 2.7 percentage points for all women 16 years and older (not seasonally adjusted).

During the current recession, the number of working-age (ages 25-54) female heads of household who are either unemployed or "marginally attached" to the labor force has increased dramatically. Marginally attached workers are those that are not counted as part of the labor force, even though they want a job, are available for work, and have searched for a job in the past 12 months. Unlike those counted as unemployed, marginally attached workers have not searched for work in the preceding 4 weeks. (See Figure 3) The increase in the number of marginally attached female heads of household has occurred across all demographic groups. Given that a female head of household is the sole breadwinner for her family, the growing rate of marginal labor force attachment among this group is particularly troublesome.

Nearly one million working age female heads of household wanted a job but could not find one as of April 2009, 16 months into the recession.[5] These included 761,000 unemployed working- age heads of household, 304,000 more than at the start of the recession, and an additional 154,000 "marginally attached", 92,000 more than at the start of the recession.[6]

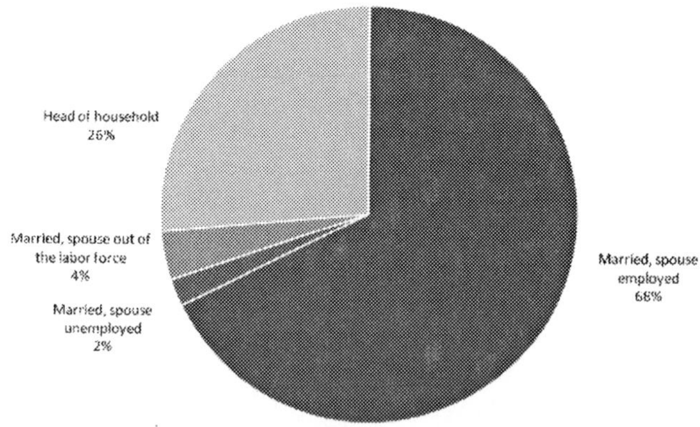

Source: JEC calculations based on data from the Bureau of Labor Statistics, Current Population Survey.

Figure 2. Nearly One-Third of Working Moms Are Their Families' Sole Earner Employed Women in the Labor Force with Children Under 18 Years Old, 2008 Annual Averages

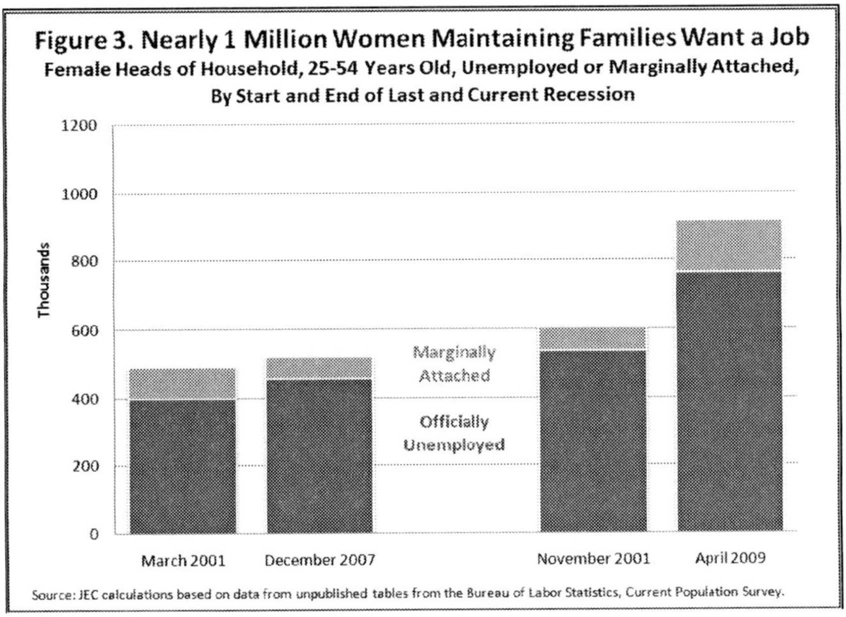

The unemployment rate today for all female heads of households is 10.0 percent, which exceeds the highest rate (9.0 percent) experienced during the 2001 recession and the "jobless recovery" that followed. Because employment for female heads of household never regained strength during the jobless recovery of the 2000s, this group entered the current recession with a relatively high unemployment rate as compared to the rest of the population.[7] (See Figure 4) In December 2007, the overall civilian unemployment rate was 4.9 percent[8] while the rate for female heads of household was 6.9 percent.[9]

Comparing the current recession to the 2001 recession shows how much more severe this recession is for female heads of household. While the unemployment rates were similar at the start of the recession, the duration of the current recession is taking a heavy toll. Over the past 12 months, the unemployment rate among all female heads of household has steadily climbed by 3.2 percentage points, to its current level of 10.0 percent. One out of every ten women maintaining a family is unemployed.[10] (See Figure 4)

Women of Color Are Faring the Worst in this Recession

White women, including white female heads of household, have fared somewhat better than women of color. In both recessions these households experienced a fairly steady, although high, rate of unemployment. (See Figure 5) But the current recession now has this group facing an unemployment rate of 8.7 percent, 3.1 percentages points higher than one year ago and considerably higher than at any point during the 2001 recession.[11]

Figure 4. Unemployment Rate Among All Female Heads of Household
By Month for Last and Current Recession

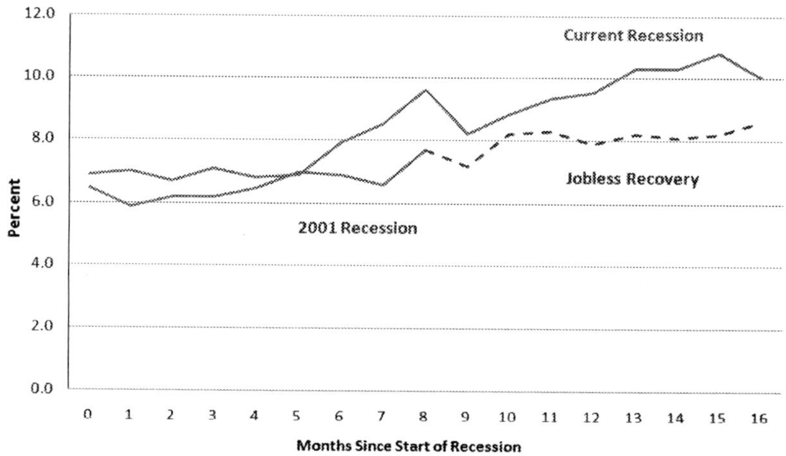

Source: JEC calculations based on non-seasonally adjusted data from unpublished tables from the Bureau of Labor Statistics, Current Population Survey.

Figure 5. Unemployment Rate Among White Female Heads of Household
By Month for Last and Current Recession

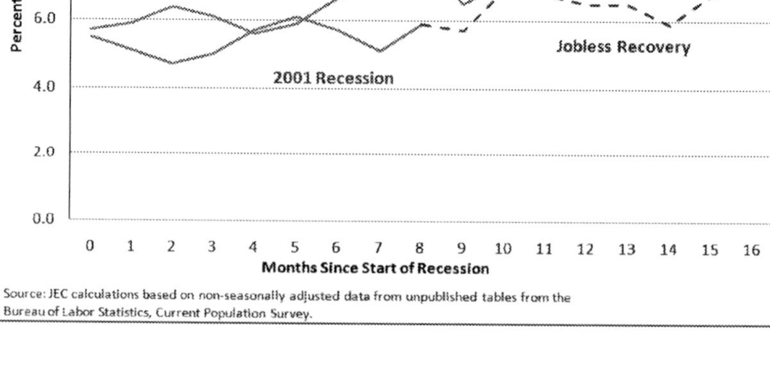

Source: JEC calculations based on non-seasonally adjusted data from unpublished tables from the Bureau of Labor Statistics, Current Population Survey.

Figure 6. Unemployment Rate Among Black Female Heads of Household
By Month for Last and Current Recession

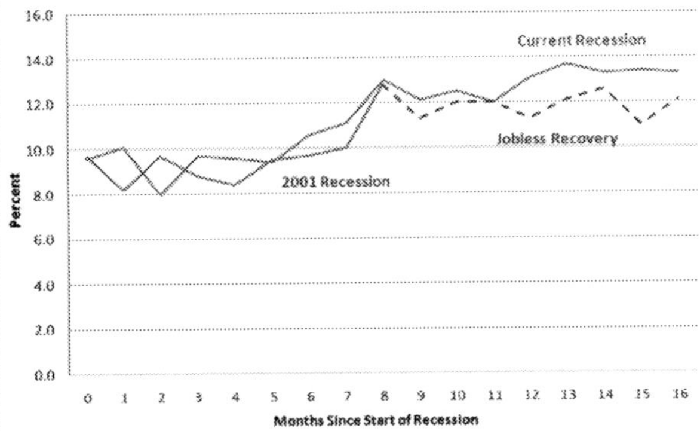

Source: JEC calculations based on non-seasonally adjusted data from unpublished tables from the Bureau of Labor Statistics, Current Population Survey.

Black female heads of household started both recessions with an unemployment rate just under 10 percent, well above the average for all female heads of household.[12] (See Figure 6) At first, their experience in the labor market during this recession was comparable to their experience in the 2001 recession. However, as the current recession intensified, the gap widened between the unemployment rates in the current recession and in the jobless recovery following the 2001 recession. The unemployment rate for black female heads of household is currently 3.7 percentage points higher than it was one year ago, suggesting that the employment situation for these women is quite difficult.

Hispanic female heads of household started this recession with a lower unemployment rate than in 2001. (See Figure 7) Over the past 12 months, the unemployment rate for Hispanic female heads of household has increased 4.0 percentage points.[13]

SUMMARY

The American Recovery and Reinvestment Act (ARRA) will temper the effects of the current recession for these families right now and over time. Extended unemployment benefits, nutrition assistance programs, preserving Medicaid benefits and tax cuts will bring immediate relief for these families. In addition, ARRA invests in job creation in education, healthcare, and child care that tend to disproportionately employ women. This will help to ensure that female-headed households will not be left behind in the recovery.

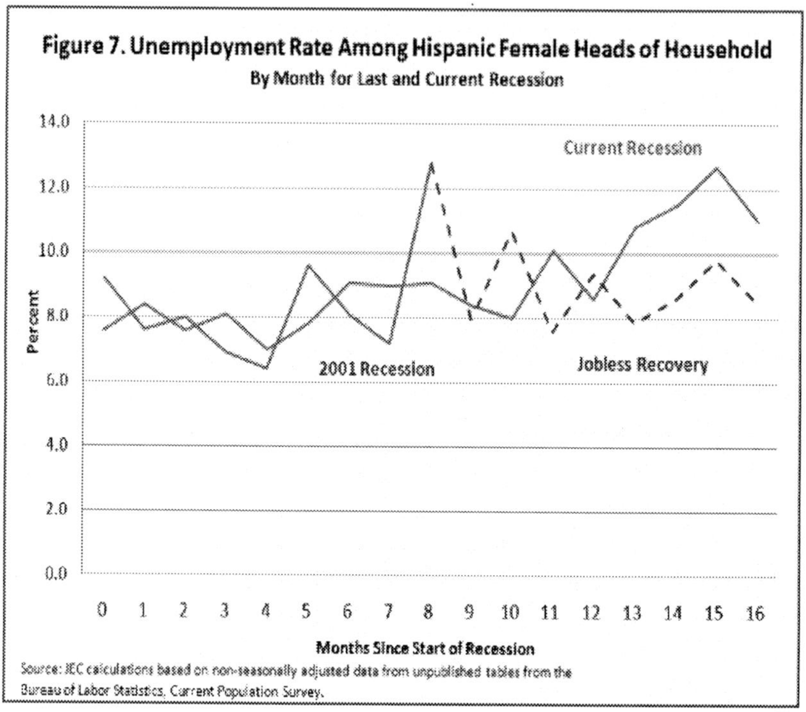

End Notes

[1] Joint Economic Committee, "Equality in Job Loss: Women Are Increasingly Vulnerable to Layoffs During Recessions" July 22, 2008.

[2] Bureau of Labor Statistics (BLS), Current Population Survey (CPS), Table 4. Number of families by presence and age of own children under 18 years old, type of family, employment status of parents, race and Hispanic or Latino ethnicity, 2008 annual averages. The Current Population Survey is a monthly survey of about 50,000 households conducted by the Bureau of the Census for the Bureau of Labor Statistics. The sample is scientifically selected to represent the civilian noninstitutional population. See www.census.gov/cps/ for more information on this survey.

[3] BLS, Current Employment Statistics. The last seven months available data are for August 2008 through February 2009.

[4] BLS, Current Population Survey, unpublished tables. These data are not seasonally adjusted. According to the CPS, a "family" is a group of two persons or more (one of whom is the head of the household) residing together and related by birth, marriage, or adoption. Thus, female heads of households may include households where the dependents are the aging parents rather than children of the head of household. We note that the CPS discontinued the use of the word "head of household" in March 1980 and replaced it with "householder."

[5] This is the sum of the unemployed and the marginally attached. *Ibid.*

[6] *Ibid.*

[7] *Ibid.*

[8] BLS, Current Population Survey, Table A-1. Employment status of the civilian population by sex and age, various months. These data are seasonally adjusted.

[9] BLS, Current Population Survey, unpublished tables.

[10] *Ibid.* We note that the April 2009 data show a reduction in the unemployment rate. However, this is a highly volatile series and it is not possible to extrapolate a change in trend from a single observation. This hold for figures 4-7.

[11] *Ibid.*

[12] *Ibid.*

[13] Although none of the data used for Figures 4 -7 are seasonally adjusted, a seasonal trend is only visible for Hispanic female heads of households, shown in Figure 7. The peak in the unemployment rate during the last recession and the spike in unemployment during month 12 of the current recession are for December. This strong seasonality may indicate that Hispanic women who maintain families are more likely to be employed in occupations that have strong seasonal trends. *Ibid.*

In: Unemployment: A Closer Look
Editors: Jacob S. Mlakar
ISBN: 978-1-61122-762-8

Chapter 8

UNDERSTANDING THE ECONOMY: LONG-TERM UNEMPLOYMENT IN THE AFRICAN AMERICAN COMMUNITY

Carolyn B. Maloney

EXECUTIVE SUMMARY

This report provides an in-depth look at unemployment, including long-term unemployment, among African American or black workers. Since 1972, when the Bureau of Labor Statistics started tracking unemployment rates by race, it has become clear that the overall unemployment rate for the United States has masked the depth of the unemployment problem within the African American community.

This report is the first in a series of Joint Economic Committee reports examining the unemployment situation among different demographic groups. It shows that while African American workers have historically faced rates of unemployment and long-term unemployment higher than the overall rate, the unemployment problems in the African American community were exacerbated during the Great Recession. Additionally, a larger percentage of African Americans are currently "marginally attached" or have dropped out of the work force, relative to the population as a whole.[1]

Specifically, this report shows that:

- The current unemployment rate for African Americans is over 6 percentage points higher than the overall unemployment rate.
- African American men have been especially hit during this recession, with nearly 1 in 5 facing unemployment.
- African American women have seen their unemployment rate jump from 7.1 percent in February 2007 to 13.1 percent in February 2010. Moreover, African American female heads of household, who bear the sole financial responsibility for their families, have an even higher unemployment rate of 15.0 percent.
- African American workers of all ages are experiencing higher unemployment rates than the overall population, but younger workers have been especially hard hit during this recession. More than 2 out of 5 African American teenagers are unemployed, compared to an overall teen unemployment rate of slightly over 25 percent.
- While having at least a college degree has usually been an effective shield against unemployment, African Americans with a 4-year college degree have an unemployment rate of 8.2 percent, almost double the unemployment rate for white workers (4.5 percent) with a similar level of education.
- African Americans have experienced longer stretches of unemployment than the general population. Although African American workers make up only 11.5 percent of the labor force, they account for more than 20 percent of the long-term unemployed, and make up 22 percent of workers who have been unemployed for over a year. The median duration of unemployment for African American workers has risen from less than 3 months before the recession began to almost six months.
- Finally, using an alternative measure of unemployment and underemployment, this report shows that one in four African Americans faces underemployment or unemployment.

Understanding the employment challenges facing the African American community is just one important part of the process of devising effective policies to reduce unemployment for workers in all demographic groups. Longer durations of unemployment and higher unemployment rates could be symptomatic of a mismatch between skills and available jobs and may require more targeted policy actions to correct. Unemployment among teenagers is especially troubling, as economists have found that spells of unemployment among youth may lead to lower future wages and poorer career trajectories.[2]

Thus, in addition to reducing the unemployment rate, policymakers must also consider ways of limiting the long-term impact of the recession on workers who have been unemployed for extended periods of time to make sure that these workers can move into employment.

The following charts show that blacks or African Americans have historically faced rates of unemployment higher than the overall rate, regardless of age, sex, or education. While workers across the United States were hard hit during the Great Recession, the problems facing black or African American workers have been even greater, especially among the long-term unemployed.

A higher-than-average rate of unemployment has been a persistent problem within the black or African American community. Going back as far as 1972, when the Bureau of Labor Statistics began keeping track of unemployment rates by race, the unemployment rate of African Americans aged 16 and over has consistently been at least 50 percent higher than the overall unemployment rate. At times, it has been more than double. During the most recent recession, which began in December 2007, the unemployment rate of African Americans climbed from 9.0 percent to a quarter-century high of 16.5 percent. While the unemployment rate edged down to 15.8 in February 2010, the unemployment rate for African Americans is still over 6 percentage points higher than the general population, the largest gap since February 1994 (excluding the Great Recession).

Chart 1. Unemployment Is Persistently Higher In the Black Community

Unemployment Rate (Seasonally Adjusted)

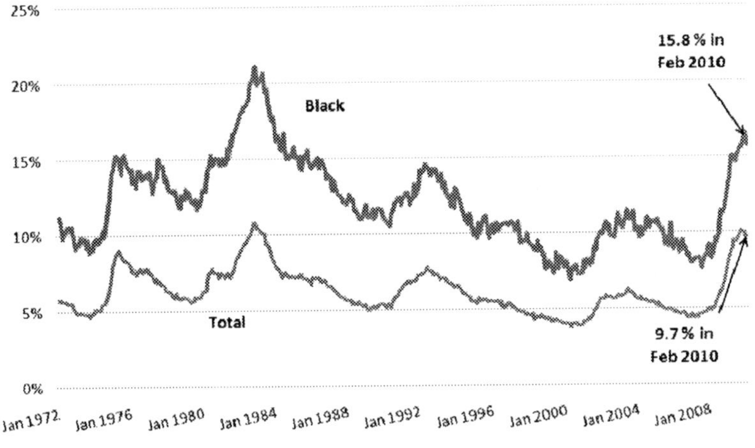

Source: Bureau of Labor Statistics.

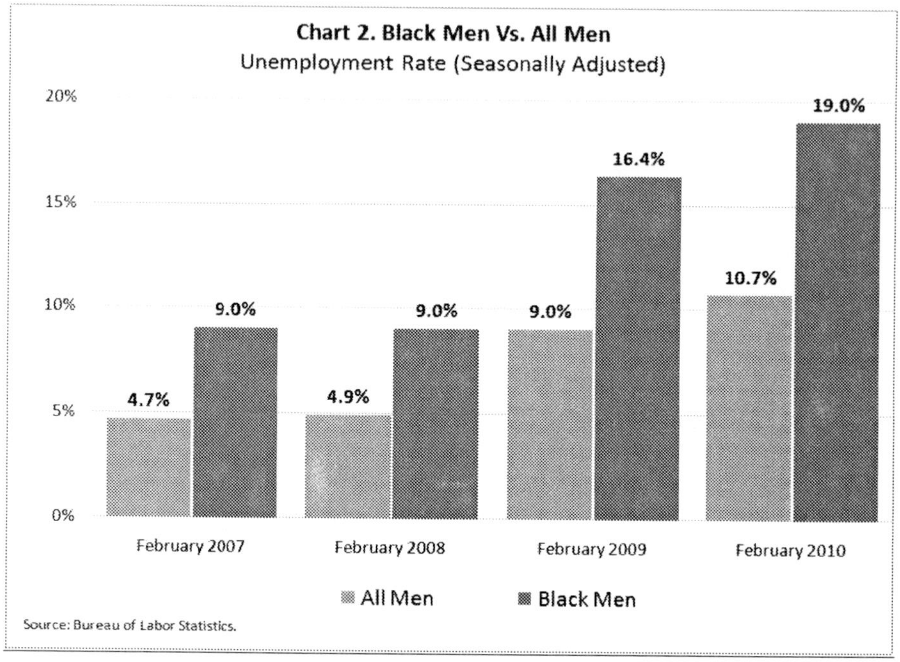
Chart 2. Black Men Vs. All Men
Unemployment Rate (Seasonally Adjusted)
20%
15%
10%
5%
0%
4.7%
9.0%
4.9%
9.0%
9.0%
16.4%
10.7%
19.0%
February 2007
February 2008
February 2009
February 2010
All Men
Black Men
Source: Bureau of Labor Statistics.

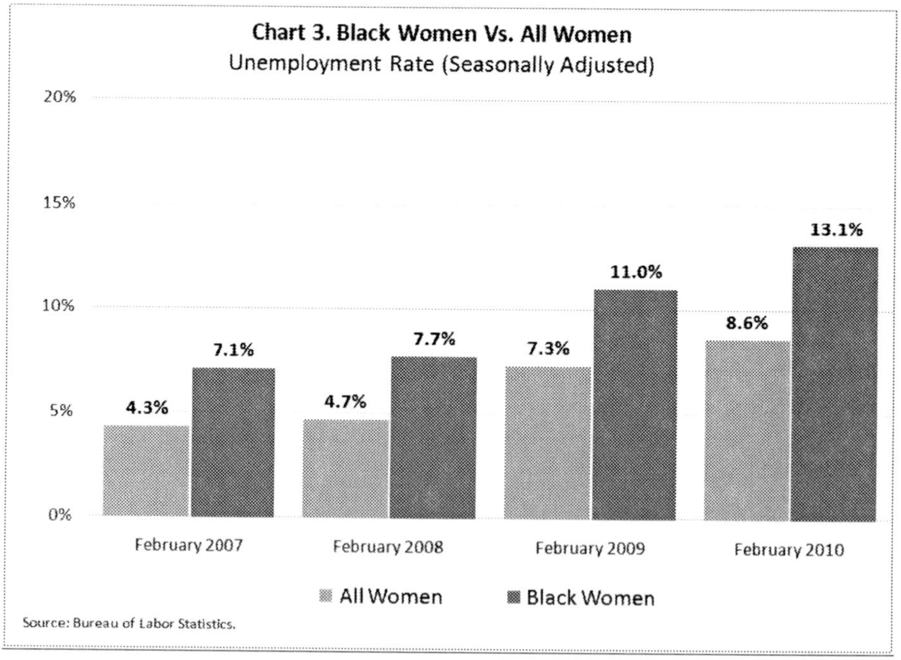
Chart 3. Black Women Vs. All Women
Unemployment Rate (Seasonally Adjusted)
20%
15%
10%
5%
0%
4.3%
7.1%
4.7%
7.7%
7.3%
11.0%
8.6%
13.1%
February 2007
February 2008
February 2009
February 2010
All Women
Black Women
Source: Bureau of Labor Statistics.

Unemployment rates are traditionally higher among men than among women. Since the recession began, African American men have seen their rate of unemployment rise to startling levels. The disparity between this rate and the overall unemployment rate of men has grown substantially as well. While the unemployment rate for all men rose 6 percentage points to 10.7 between February 2007 and February 2010, the jobless rate for African American men climbed a full 10.0 percentage points, reaching 19.0 percent in February 2010.

Like African American men, African American women also experienced jobless rates well above those for all women prior to the start of the current recession. In February 2007, the unemployment rate among African American women aged 16 and older was 7.1 percent, compared to 4.3 percent among all women aged 16 and older. Most recently, the jobless rate for African American women of 13.1 percent in February 2010 was 4.5 percentage points higher than the unemployment rate for all women.

Among women workers, African American female heads of household face particularly high rates of unemployment. This high rate is especially troubling because female heads of household bear sole financial responsibility for families. The implications of high unemployment rates among this population may have long-term consequences on the educational attainment of children in these households.

Chart 4. All Women Heads of Household Vs. Black Women Heads of Household
Unemployment Rate, February 2010 (Not Seasonally Adjusted)

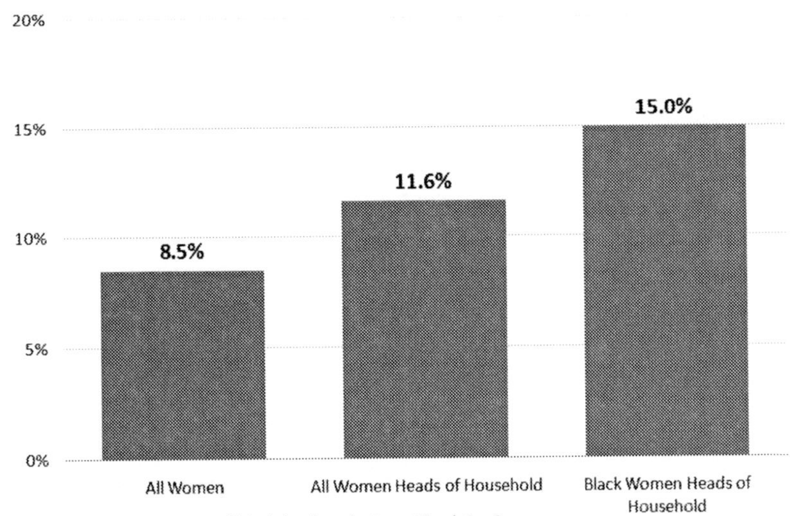

Source: Bureau of Labor Statistics, unpublished data from the Current Population Survey.

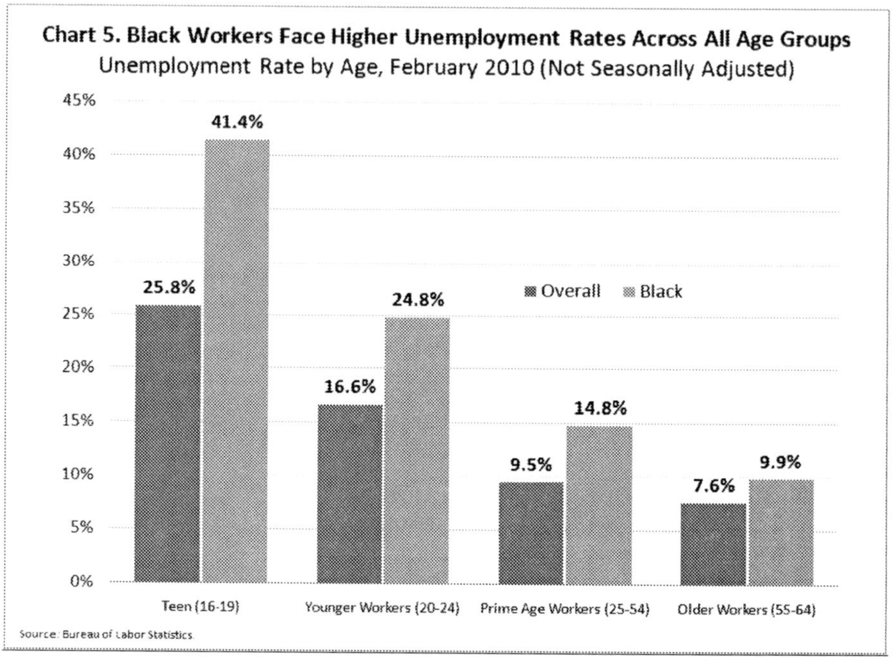

The weak labor market has hit African American workers of all age groups much more heavily than it has hit the overall labor force. In February 2010, a staggering 41.4 percent of African American teens (those between ages 16 to 19) were unemployed, 15.6 percent higher than the overall teen unemployment rate of 25.8 percent. A similar pattern emerges when comparing African American and overall unemployment rates across various age groups. Among younger African American workers (those between ages 20 and 24), 24.8 percent were unemployed, compared to the overall unemployment rate of younger workers, 16.6 percent. Prime age African American workers (those between the ages of 25 and 54) had an unemployment rate of 14.8 percent, 5.3 percent higher than the overall unemployment rate of prime age workers, which was 9.5 percent. Older workers (those between the ages of 55 and 64) had an unemployment rate of 9.9 percent, slightly higher than the overall unemployment rate of older workers, which was 7.6 percent.

While having at least a college degree has usually been an effective shield against unemployment, African Americans with a 4-year college degree are experiencing unemployment rates of 8.2 percent, almost double the unemployment rate for white workers (4.5 percent) with a similar level of education. Between February 2007 and February 2010, the unemployment rate for African American workers with a 4-year college degree increased 263 percent, compared to 150 percent for white workers with a 4-year degree.

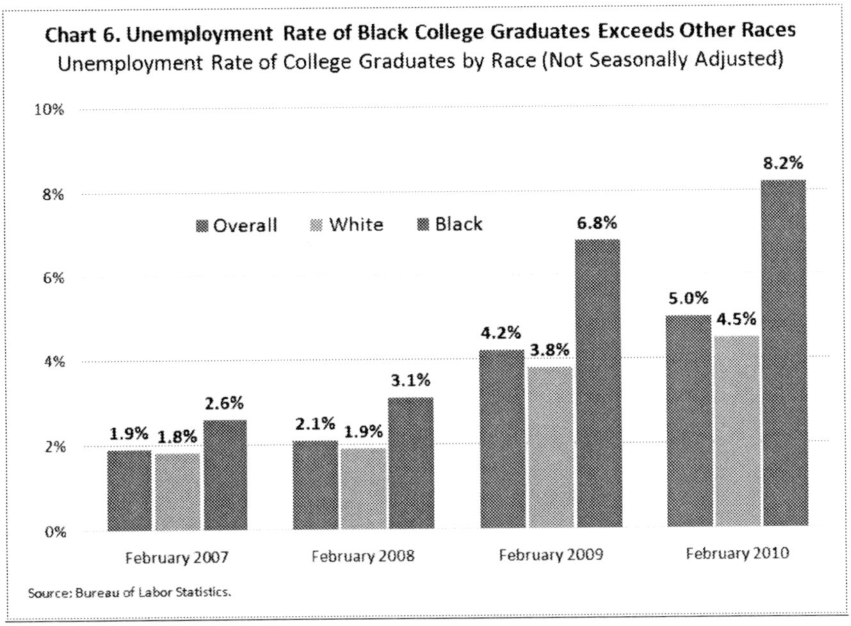

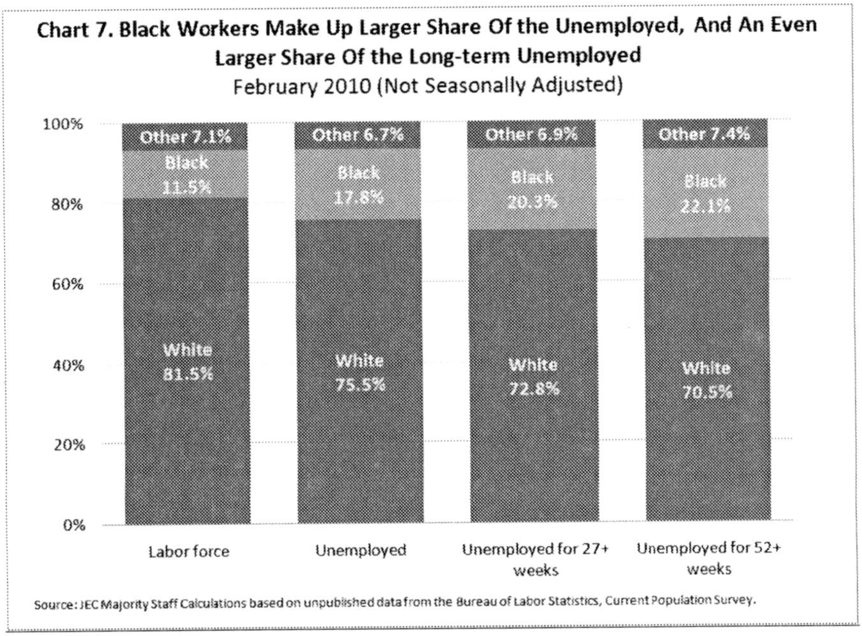

Although African American workers make up 11.5 percent of the total civilian labor force, they are overrepresented among the unemployed and made up 17.8 percent of the total number of unemployed workers as of February 2010. When one examines the composition of long-term unemployed workers, however, the picture is even more troubling. African Americans make up one-fifth (20.3 percent) of long-term unemployed workers, which means they have been jobless for 27 or more weeks. In addition, they account for 22.1 percent of workers who have been unemployed for 52 or more weeks. These numbers underscore the disproportionate impact of the recession on African American workers and the need for job creation policies that target the long-term unemployed. There are a number of reasons why unemployment may elude a substantial number of long-term unemployed workers. Workers who lost their jobs at the start of the recession may be the least skilled and any skills they had may have deteriorated during a long spell of unemployment. Or, these workers may have been employed in shrinking sectors of the economy – such as construction or manufacturing – and may not have the skills needed to move to the expanding sectors of the economy, such as the healthcare sector.

Chart 8. 45% of Jobless Black Workers Have Been Unemployed For 27 Weeks Or Longer
Distribution of Duration of Unemployment for Black Workers
February 2010 (Not Seasonally Adjusted)

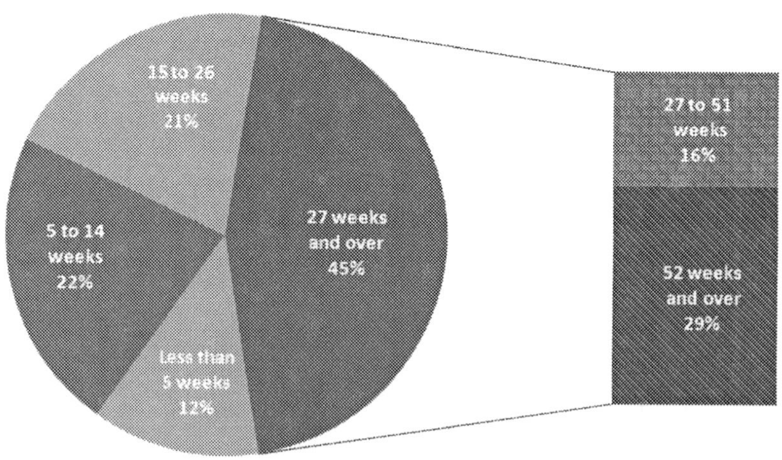

Source: JEC Majority Staff Calculations based on unpublished data from the Bureau of Labor Statistics, Current Population Survey.

In February 2010, a substantial fraction—45 percent—of unemployed African American workers had been unemployed for 27 or more weeks. In contrast, 39.3 percent of all unemployed workers had been unemployed for 27 or more weeks. Looking deeper, 16 percent of unemployed African American workers had been jobless for between 27 and 51 weeks, and 29 percent had been without work for 52 or more weeks. This highlights the fact that most long-term unemployed workers—over 60 percent—had been unemployed for more than a year.

For the month of February 2007—before the Great Recession began—the median duration of unemployment among jobless African American workers (11.2 weeks) was already higher than the median duration of unemployment for the overall population of unemployed workers (8.8 weeks). Since then, the median duration of unemployment for African Americans has climbed, as has the disparity. In a span of three years—from February 2007 to February 2010—the median duration of unemployed African American workers more than doubled to 23.8 weeks. During the same time span, the gap in median unemployment duration between unemployed African American workers and all unemployed workers also rose, from 2.4 weeks to 4.2 weeks; the gap between unemployed African American and white workers, 5.4 weeks, is even higher.

Chart 9. The Typical Unemployment Spell For A Black Worker Lasts 23.8 Weeks
Median Duration of Unemployment (Not Seasonally Adjusted)

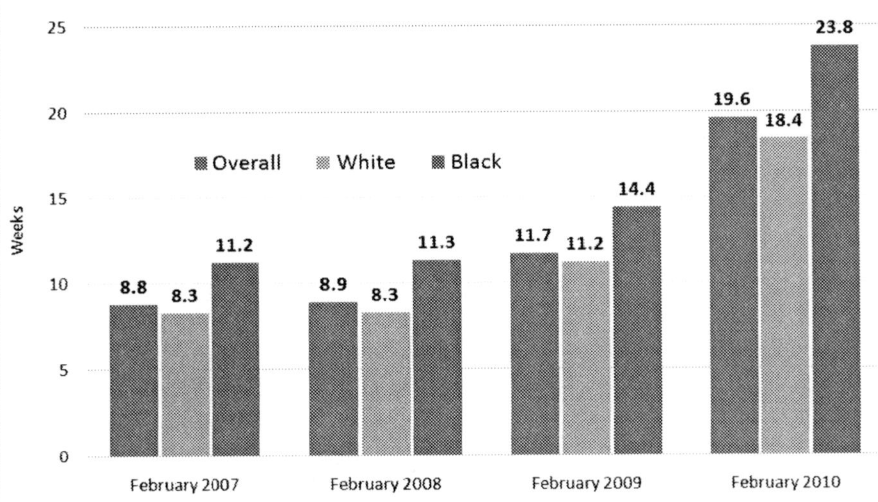

Source: Bureau of Labor Statistics.

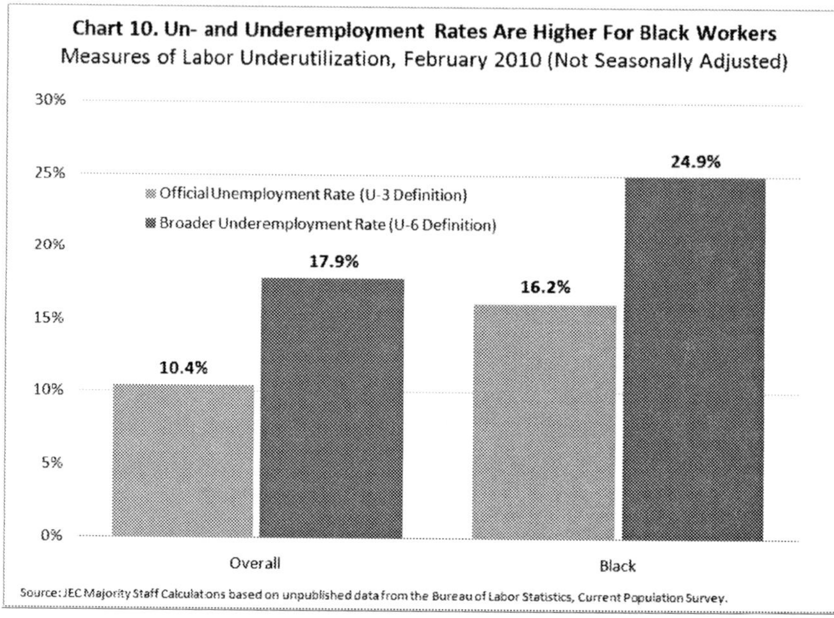

Although the unemployment rate is the most common measure of the state of the labor market, a broader measure is the U-6 rate, which includes the underemployed. It takes into account people who are marginally attached—those not included in the labor force who want a job, are available to work, and have looked for a job at some point in the past twelve months (but not the past four weeks)—and workers who are part-time for economic reasons, meaning that they have part-time jobs but would like full-time work. The graph above shows that African Americans have had a U-6 rate significantly higher than the overall population. In February 2008, the U-6 rate for African Americans was 14.4 percent, compared to the overall rate of 9.5 percent. By February 2010, the U-6 rate for African Americans rose by 10.5 percent to 24.9 percent, while the overall U-6 rate rose by 8.4 percent to 17.9 percent. Thus, the U-6 rate for African Americans, which had already been high at the beginning of the recession, rose more than the overall U-6 rate during this time period.

The differences in the U-6 rate between African Americans and the overall population can be attributed to higher shares of marginally attached and unemployed workers in the African American community. However, when it comes to the portion of workers who are part-time for economic reasons, there is no substantial difference between African American workers and the overall population.

Chart 11. Greater Shares of Unemployed and Marginally Attached Workers Contribute to a Higher Under-Employment Rate For Blacks During the Recession

Alternative Measures of Labor Underutilization (Not Seasonally Adjusted)

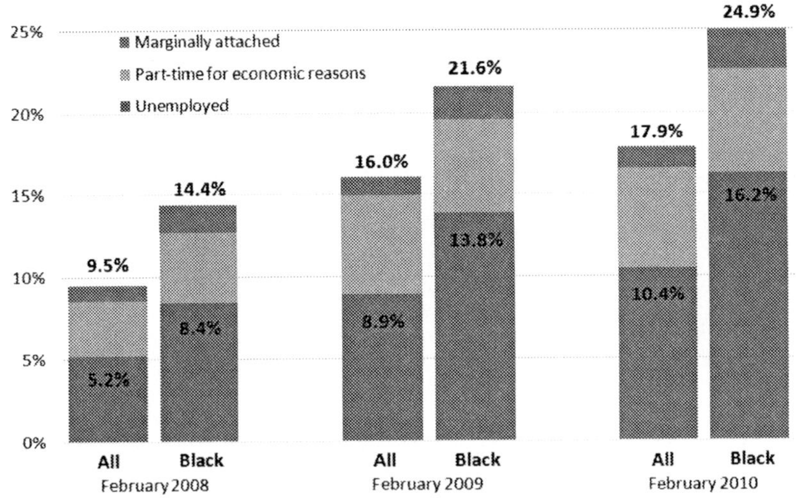

Source: JEC Majority Staff Calculations based on unpublished data from the Bureau of Labor Statistics, Current Population Survey.

CONCLUSION

This report offers a baseline understanding of the employment challenges facing the African American community, focusing on changes in unemployment and long-term unemployment over the past three years. The unemployment rate statistics are broken down by gender, age, and higher education levels. The report shows that African Americans have experienced higher rates of unemployment and longer stretches of unemployment than the general population. African American men and African American teenagers have been particularly hard hit. Furthermore, a college degree has failed to protect African Americans from unemployment.

In coming months, the JEC will provide similar reports for other demographic groups, including Hispanics, youth, and women. These reports can be a starting point for policymakers working to address the higher unemployment rates and longer durations of unemployment experienced during the Great Recession among different demographic groups. The reports also may provide a reference for further study and analysis as academics, economists, and the JEC work to understand why certain demographic groups were hit hardest in the recession and what can be done to help get them back to work.

End Notes

[1] According to the Bureau of Labor Statistics, the labor force does not include "persons under 16 years of age, all persons confined to institutions such as nursing homes and prisons, and persons on active duty in the Armed Forces." The labor force is made up of the employed and the unemployed. The remainder of the population — those who have no job and are not looking for one—are counted as "not in the labor force." Many who are not in the labor force are in school, have retired from working, or have family responsibilities that keep them out of the labor force.

"Marginally attached" workers are not in the labor force, but would like a job and are available for work. In order to be counting as "marginally attached" to the labor force, a person must also have looked for work in the last 12 months.

[2] See, eg., Philip Oreopoulous, et al., "The Short- and Long-Term Career Effects of Graduating in a Recession: Hysteresis and Heterogeneity in the Market for College Graduates," working paper, (updated National Bureau of Economics Working Paper No. 12159), available online at http://www.columbia.edu/~vw2112/papers/cyclupgroreovonwaheisz.pdf, and Thomas A. Mroz and Timothy H. Savage, "The Long-Term Effects of Youth Unemployment," *The Journal of Human Resources*, Spring 2006, pp. 259- 293.

In: Unemployment: A Closer Look
Editors: Jacob S. Mlakar
ISBN: 978-1-61122-762-8

Chapter 9

UNDERSTANDING THE ECONOMY: UNEMPLOYMENT IN THE HISPANIC COMMUNITY

Carolyn B. Maloney

EXECUTIVE SUMMARY

Workers across the United States have been hard hit during the "Great Recession," but in many respects, workers of Latino or Hispanic ethnicity are facing even greater employment challenges.[1] Latinos make up over one-seventh (14.8 percent) of the U.S. labor force, but represented almost one- fifth (19.0 percent) of the unemployed in March 2010.

Rising unemployment in the Latino community appears to be caused in large part by the bursting of the housing bubble. Employment in the construction sector reached a peak of 7.7 million workers in August 2006. By February 2010, however, employment had plummeted to 5.6 million workers - a 27.8 percent drop. As this report shows, Latino workers are over-represented in the sectors that contracted the most during the recession, including the construction industry.

- In 2007, 14.7 percent of Hispanic workers were employed in the construction sector compared to 8.1 percent of the overall labor force.

- By 2009, only 11.6 percent of Hispanic workers were employed in the construction sector compared to 6.9 percent of the overall labor force.
- Latinos are also over-represented in two other sectors that were hit hard during this recession: the manufacturing sector and the leisure and hospitality sector. Manufacturing employment fell by 16 percent and employment in the leisure and hospitality sector fell by 4 percent from December 2007 to December 2009. In 2007, 11.6 percent of the Hispanic workforce was employed in the manufacturing sector compared to 11.2 percent of the overall population, and 11.8 percent of the Hispanic workforce was employed in leisure and hospitality sector compared to 8.5 percent of the overall population.
- In 2007, Latinos were under-represented in the only sector that expanded during the recession, the education and health services sector. In 2007, 21 percent of the labor force was employed in the education and health services sector compared to 14.4 percent of the Latino workforce.

Furthermore, large concentrations of Latino workers live in the states that were hardest hit by the collapse of the housing market – Nevada, Arizona, Florida and California. The freefall in house prices placed further strains on the construction sector in those states.

- Most states with higher percentages of Latino workers were severely impacted by the collapse of the housing market. While home prices nationwide fell 30.8 percent from the peak in March 2006 to April 2009,[2] home prices in Nevada, Arizona, Florida, and California fell by much more than the national average.[3] Only two states with large Latino populations, Texas and New Mexico, saw smaller home price declines and lower foreclosure rates than the national average.[4]
- At the same time, Nevada, Arizona, Florida, and California saw large increases in foreclosure rates. In the first quarter of 2007, foreclosure rates in these states were under 1.2 percent of mortgages, but foreclosure rates increased rapidly.[5] For example, by the end of 2009, the foreclosure rate was 9.8 percent in Nevada and 13.4 percent in Florida, while the national foreclosure rate was 4.6 percent.

Until the collapse of the housing market, Hispanic workers were facing unemployment rates similar to the overall population. The gains made in reducing the unemployment rate for Hispanic workers quickly evaporated with the Great Recession, with the unemployment rate for Hispanic workers rising to 13.1 percent in October 2009, 3 percentage points higher than the 10.1 percent overall unemployment rate.

Policies to create jobs during the recovery must ensure that the unemployment rate drops for all workers, regardless of race or ethnicity. Because Hispanic workers are over-represented in certain industries that either may not be expanding or may grow slowly during the recovery, targeted policies to make sure that these workers have the skills to move into expanding sectors may be necessary. Additional policies to encourage mobility of the labor force from states still experiencing a housing slump may also be warranted.

BACKGROUND

Since the Bureau of Labor Statistics began tracking unemployment rates by race and ethnicity, the unemployment rate for Hispanic workers has been consistently higher than the overall unemployment rate [see Figure 1]. Despite the relative difficulties faced by Hispanic workers, there was reason to be optimistic in May 2006, as the gap between the Hispanic unemployment rate (4.9 percent) and the overall unemployment rate (4.6 percent) reached a record low of 0.3 percentage points. Coinciding with the steady progress made by Hispanic workers—many of whom were employed in the construction industry—was the boom in the housing market, with home prices peaking in mid-2006. However, when home prices started plummeting from their peak and the housing market began its collapse, the gains made by Hispanics evaporated. By October 2009—three and half years after the disparity between the unemployment rates of Hispanics and the rest of the population reached its low point—the Hispanic unemployment rate climbed to 13.1 percent, 3 percentage points higher than the overall unemployment rate of 10.1 percent. While the disparity has dropped slightly in the last few months, the Hispanic unemployment rate in March 2010 was 12.6 percent, 2.9 percentage points higher than the overall unemployment rate of 9.7 percent. In absolute terms, out of the 22.7 million Hispanics that comprised the U.S. labor force (14.8 percent of the total) in March, 2.9 million were unemployed (19.1 percent of the total).

The Great Recession derailed the gains that Hispanics had achieved relative to the overall labor force. Since the housing bubble may have contributed much to the progress made by Hispanic workers, a long process of sectoral reallocation within the Hispanic labor force may be part of what is necessary for them to once again approach parity with the overall labor force.

Figure 1. Unemployment is Persistently Higher in the Hispanic Community
Unemployment Rate (Seasonally Adjusted)

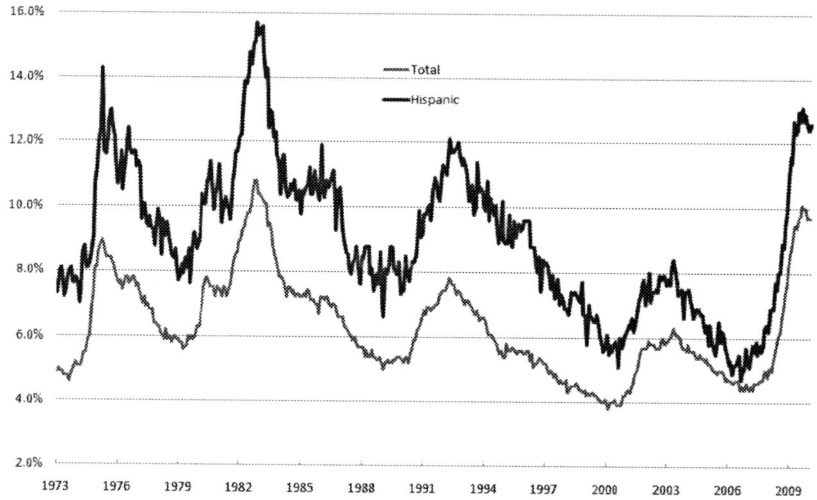

Source: Bureau of Labor Statistics.

HISPANICS FACE HIGHER UNEMPLOYMENT REGARDLESS OF GENDER AND AGE

As job losses mounted during the recession, unemployment among Hispanic men rose to troubling levels. The disparity between this rate and the overall unemployment rate of men also grew [see Figure 2]. While the unemployment rate for all men rose by 6.8 percentage points to 11.8 percent between March 2007 and March 2010, the jobless rate for Hispanic men climbed by 8.2 percentage points, reaching 13.8 percent in March 2010.

Hispanic women also experienced jobless rates higher than those for all women prior to the start of the current recession [see Figure 3]. In March 2007, the unemployment rate among Hispanic women was 5.1 percent, compared to 4.1 percent among all women. Most recently, the jobless rate for

Latinas, 12.5 percent in March 2010, was 4.2 percentage points higher than the unemployment rate for all women.

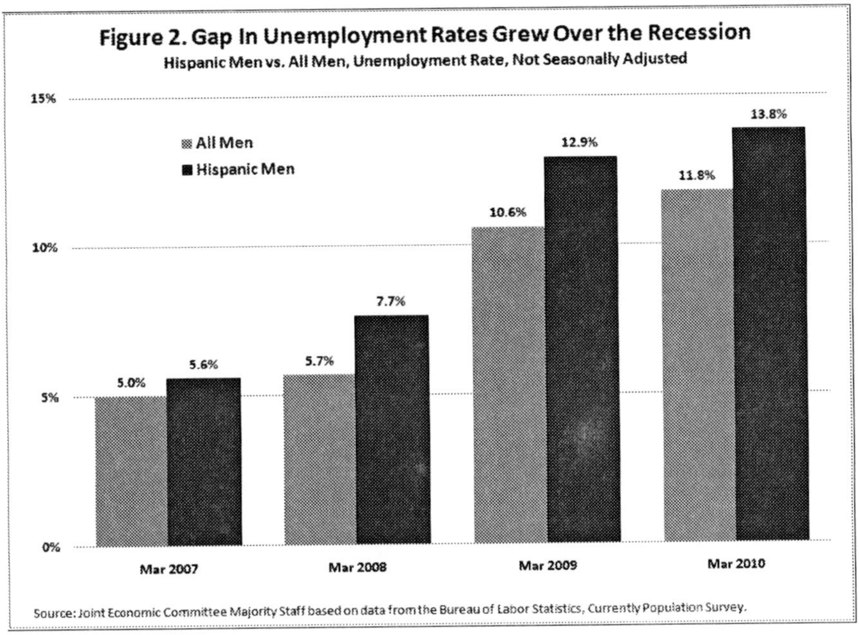

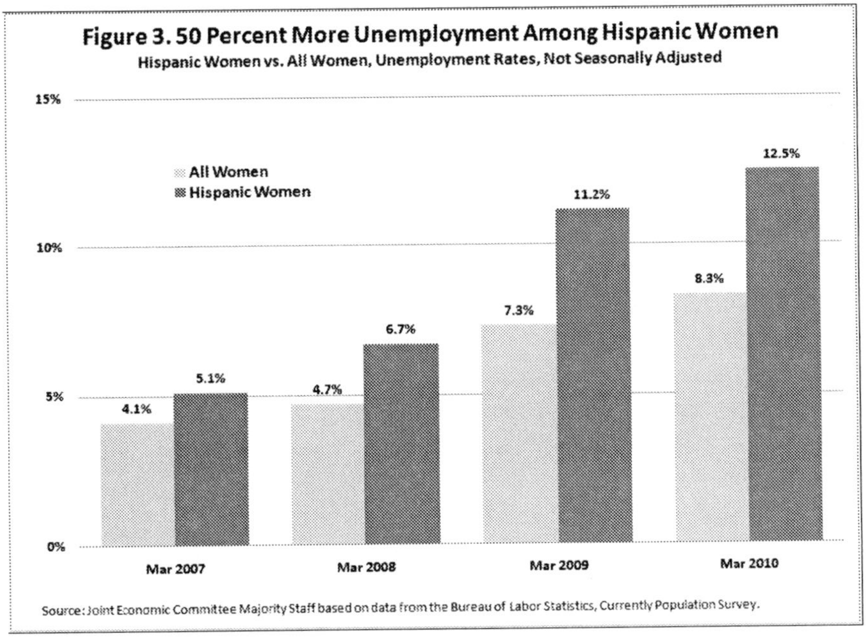

The weak labor market has hit Hispanic workers of all age groups more heavily than it has hit the overall labor force. In March 2010, nearly one-third—30.1 percent—of Hispanic teens (those between ages 16 to 19) were unemployed, compared with one-quarter (25.3 percent) of all teens. A similar pattern emerges when comparing Hispanic and overall unemployment rates across various age groups. Among younger Hispanic workers (those between ages 20 and 24), 18.2 percent were unemployed, compared to the overall unemployment rate of younger workers, 15.8 percent. Prime-age Hispanic workers (those between the ages of 25 and 54) had an unemployment rate of 11.9 percent, 2.4 percentage points higher than the overall unemployment rate of prime-age workers. Hispanic workers over 55 but under 65 had an unemployment rate of 7.3 percent compared to the unemployment rate for all workers in that age category of 9.5 percent. The largest discrepancy is among older workers (those over 65). Older Hispanic workers had an unemployment rate of 12.3 percent, compared with an overall unemployment rate of older workers of 6.9 percent. The larger gap may be attributable to the fact that Hispanic workers are more likely to be employed in occupations requiring manual labor, and employers may be less likely to fill these positions with older workers. In addition, Hispanic workers have persistently earned 25 to 31 percent less than the median weekly earnings of all employees, and these workers may not have sufficient retirement savings, and may be more likely to remain in the labor force looking for employment.[6] In the first quarter of 2010, median usual weekly earnings on Hispanic workers were $554, compared to $754 for all workers.[7]

Unemployment Spells Are Typically Shorter for Hispanics

The current economic downturn has been characterized by exceptionally long spells of unemployment. As of March 2010, 42.8 percent of the 6.7 million unemployed Americans had been out of work for 27 weeks or more, and the typical unemployment spell lasted 21.6 weeks.[8] While some demographic groups, such as African Americans, are experiencing disproportionate shares of long-term unemployment, Latinos actually experience less long-term unemployment as a share of the unemployed (38.1 percent) and shorter unemployment spells (18.9 weeks) than the overall labor force [see Figure 4]. Although the typical duration of unemployment remains at a record high for Hispanics, unemployed Hispanic workers have, at least to date, either managed to secure new work more quickly or drop out of the labor force more than other workers.

There are a number of reasons that employment remains elusive for a substantial number of long-term unemployed Hispanic workers. These workers were likely to have been employed in shrinking sectors of the economy – such as construction or manufacturing – and may not have had the skills needed to move to the expanding sectors of the economy, such as the healthcare sector. Workers who lost their jobs at the start of the recession may have been the least skilled, and their skills may have deteriorated during a long spell of unemployment.

ONE-QUARTER OF THE HISPANIC LABOR FORCE IS UNDEREMPLOYED

The official unemployment rate understates problems facing Latinos in the labor force. An alternative underemployment measure known as the "U-6" starts with the traditional unemployment rate and includes workers who are working part time but would prefer to be working full time. These workers, the involuntary part-timers, may have looked for full-time work and have been unable to find it or have had their hours cut at their current job. In addition, the U-6 also includes workers who would like a job, are available to work, and have looked for work in the last year, but they are not considered part of the labor force because they stopped looking for work over a month ago – they are known as "marginally attached workers."

As Figure 5 shows, the traditional unemployment rate masks the high rate of underemployment in the Latino labor force. In March 2010, Latino workers had an unemployment rate of 13.3 percent, 3.1 percentage points higher than the overall unemployment rate of 10.2 percent (comparing seasonally unadjusted data). However, the U-6 or underemployment rate for Latino workers was 25.1 percent, 11.8 percentage points higher than the conventional unemployment rate. For the overall labor force, the U-6 rate was 17.5 percent, which is 7.3 percentage points higher than the conventional unemployment rate. The differences in the U-6 rate between Hispanics and the overall population can be attributed to the higher share of unemployed and involuntary part-time workers in the Hispanic community [see Figure 6]. However, when it comes to the portion of workers who are marginally attached to the labor force, there is no substantial difference between Hispanic workers and the overall population. The larger gap between the traditional unemployment rate and the broader U-6 rate among Hispanics suggests that while underemployment is inarguably a significant problem for the overall labor force, it is an even greater problem for the Hispanic community.

Figure 4. Unemployment Spells Are Shorter Among Hispanic Workers
Distribution of Unemployed Workers by Duration of Unemployment, March 2010

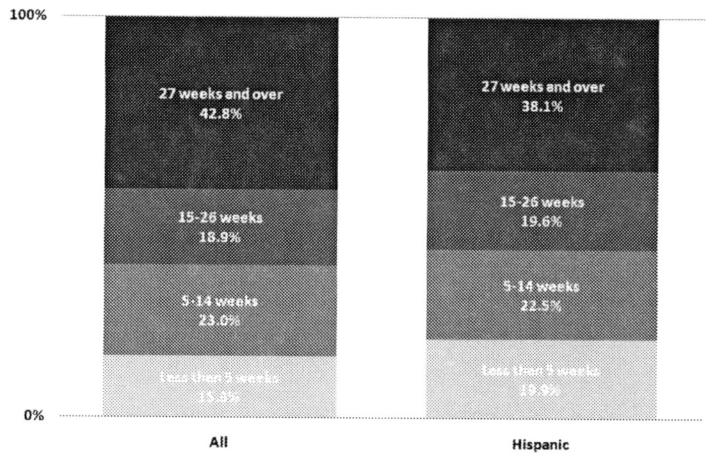

Source: Joint Economic Committee Majority Staff based on data from the Bureau of Labor Statistics.

Figure 5. Un- and Underemployment Rates Are Higher for Hispanic Workers
Measures of Labor Underutilization, March 2010 (Not Seasonally Adjusted)

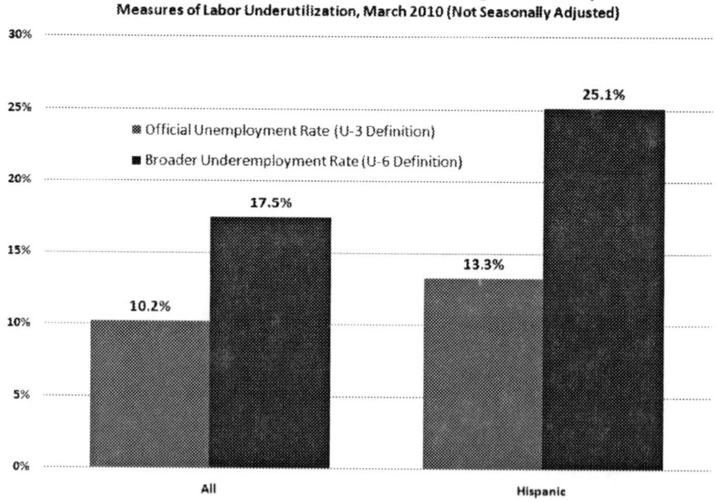

Source: Joint Economic Committee Majority Staff based on unpublished data from the Bureau of Labor Statistics, Current Population Survey.

Figure 6. More Unemployed and Involuntary Part-Time Workers Contribute to a Higher Under-Employment Rate for Hispanics During the Recession

Alternate Measures of Labor Underutilization (Not Seasonally Adjusted)

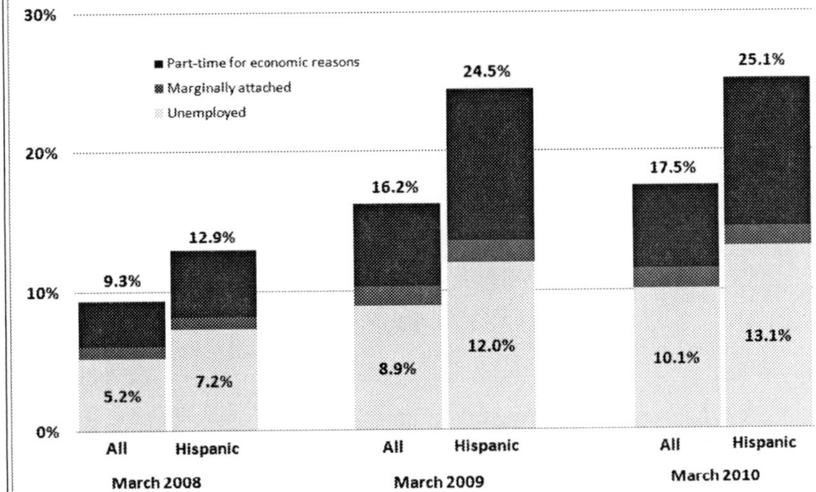

Source: JEC Majority Staff Calculations based on unpublished data from the Bureau of Labor Statistics, Current Population Survey.

HISPANIC UNEMPLOYMENT IS DRIVEN BY INDUSTRY SECTOR AND GEOGRAPHY

Prior to the start of the recession, Hispanics were more likely to work in industries such as construction, manufacturing, and leisure and hospitality – all sectors that experienced large job losses during the Great Recession [see Figure 7]. But most of the increase in the unemployment rate in the Latino community appears to be caused by the bursting of the housing bubble. Employment in the construction sector reached a peak of 7.7 million workers in August 2006.[9] By February 2010, however, employment had dropped by well over a quarter (27.8 percent) to 5.6 million workers.[10] In 2007, roughly one-in-seven (14.7 percent) Latinos worked in the construction industry, compared with one-intwelve (8.1 percent) workers in the overall labor force [see Figure 7].

Similarly, Hispanic workers were more likely to be employed in leisure and hospitality jobs, a sector that contracted by 4 percent over the course of the recession. In 2007, 11.8 percent of the Hispanic workforce was employed in leisure and hospitality sector compared to 8.5 percent of the overall labor force.

While job losses in the manufacturing sector alone may explain some of the rise in the unemployment rate among Hispanic workers, losses in the manufacturing sector do not explain the difference in the rise in unemployment between Hispanic workers and the overall labor force. While employment in the manufacturing sector fell by 16 percent from December 2007 to December 2009, Hispanic workers were only slightly over-represented in this industry sector. At the start of the recession, 11.6 percent of the Hispanic workforce was employed in the manufacturing sector compared to 11.2 percent of the overall population.

Further exacerbating unemployment during the recession, Hispanics also were significantly less likely to work in education and health services, an industry that expanded 4 percent between December 2007 and December 2009, even in the wake of widespread job losses across other sectors [see Figure 7]. In 2007, only 14.4 percent of employed Latinos were working in the education and health services industry, compared with 21.0 percent of the overall employed population.

Figure 7. Hispanic Workers Were Over-Represented in Contracting Sectors and Under-Represented in Expanding Sectors At Recession's Start

Distribution of Hispanic Employed Persons and Total Employed Persons in Selected Industries, 2007 Annual Average

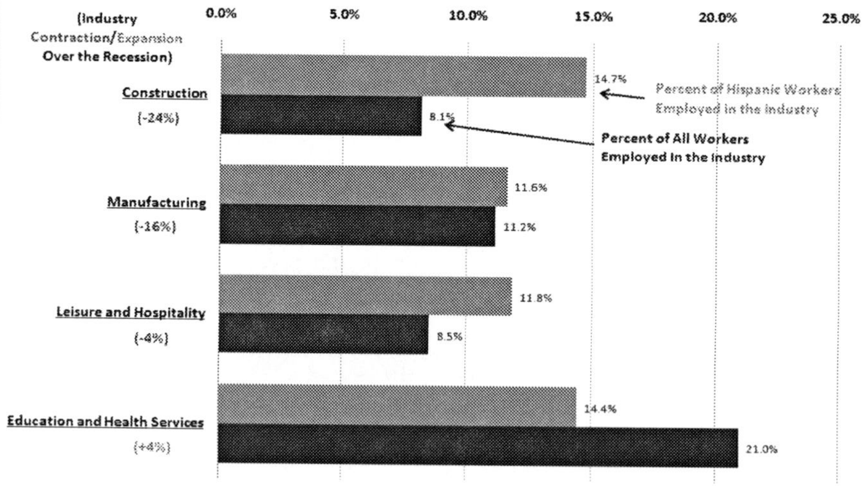

Note: Numbers in parentheses represent the percent change in employment within the industry over the recession (December 2007 to December 2009).
Source: Joint Economic Committee Majority Staff calculations based on data from the Bureau of Labor Statistics.

Figure 8. Hispanic Unemployment: Geography Matters

Percent of Hispanic Workers in Labor Force, 2009 Annual Average, and Current State Unemployment Rates

Source: JEC Majority Staff calculations based on Bureau of Labor Statistics, Current Population Survey, Preliminary 2009 Data on Employment Status by State and Demographic Group, 2009 annual averages (size of Hispanic labor force by state); for Puerto Rico: U.S. Department of Census, 2006-2008 American Community Survey 3-Year Estimates; State and Puerto Rico unemployment rates from BLS, Current Population Survey, March 2010.

Figure 9. Decline in House Prices of Selected States

Monthly Change in House Price Index, March 2006 - December 2009

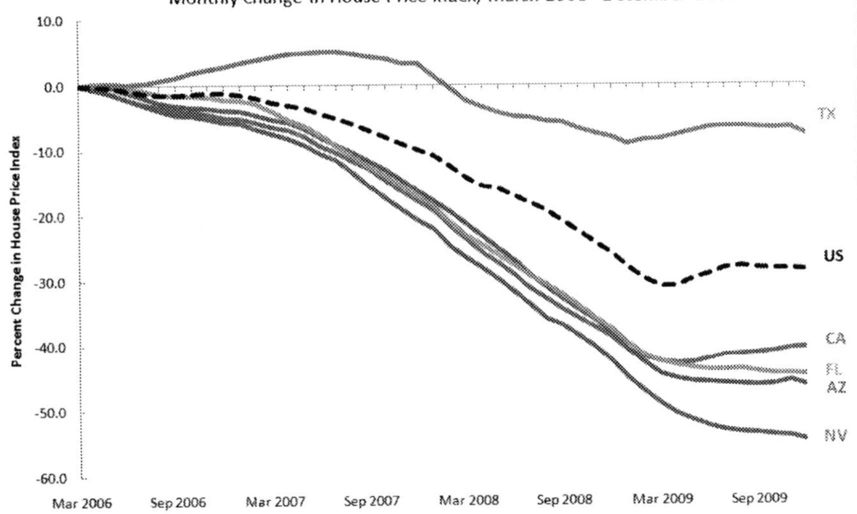

Source: Joint Economic Committee Majority Staff Calculations based on data from Loan Performance House Price Index. (Seasonally Adjusted by Haver Analytics)

Geographic differences may also explain part of the sharp rise in the Hispanic unemployment rate during this recession. Many states with large concentrations of Hispanic workers, such as California, Florida, and Nevada, have faced large employment losses and corresponding increases in the unemployment rate [see Figure 8]. These also happened to be the states that suffered tremendously from the collapse of the housing market.

While home prices nationwide fell 30.8 percent from the peak in March 2006 to the trough in April 2009,[11] home prices in Nevada, Arizona, Florida, and California fell by much more than the national average[12] [see Figure 9]. Only two states with large Latino populations, Texas and New Mexico, saw smaller home price declines and lower foreclosure rates than the national average.[13]

At the same time, Nevada, Arizona, Florida, and California saw large increases in foreclosure rates. In the first quarter of 2007, foreclosure rates in these states were under 1.2 percent, but then increased rapidly as the recession progressed.[14] For example, by the end of 2009, the foreclosure rate was 9.8 percent in Nevada and 13.4 percent in Florida, while the national foreclosure rate was 4.6 percent.

Addressing the Problems Facing Hispanic Workers

The Great Recession caused a shuffling in the distribution of Hispanic employment across industries [see Figures 10 and 11]. In 2007, Hispanics were most likely to be employed in the construction industry, but by 2009, Hispanics were most likely to be employed in the education and health activities and wholesale and retail trade sectors. Construction dropped to fourth most-common industry of employment.

Policies to create jobs during the recovery must ensure that the unemployment rate drops for all workers, regardless of race or ethnicity. Hispanic workers are over-represented in certain industries that either may not be expanding or may grow slowly during the recovery, and targeted policies to make sure that these workers have the skills to move into expanding sectors may be necessary. Additional policies to encourage mobility of the labor force from states still experiencing a housing slump may also be warranted. Members of the Hispanic community will undoubtedly benefit from job-creation and training policies that are designed to reduce unemployment, but policies that target specific sectors and regions may be more effective at combating Hispanic unemployment.

Figure 10. Distribution Employment by Industry in 2007
Distribution of Hispanic Employed Persons and Total Employed Persons
2007 Annual Averages

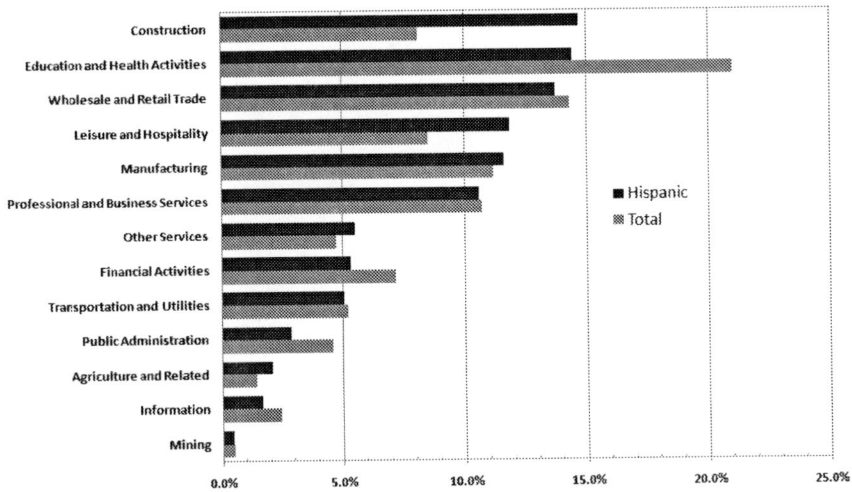

Source: JEC Majority Staff calculations based on data from the Bureau of Labor Statistics.

Figure 11. Distribution of Employment by Industry in 2009
Distribution of Hispanic Employed Persons and Total Employed Persons
2009 Annual Averages

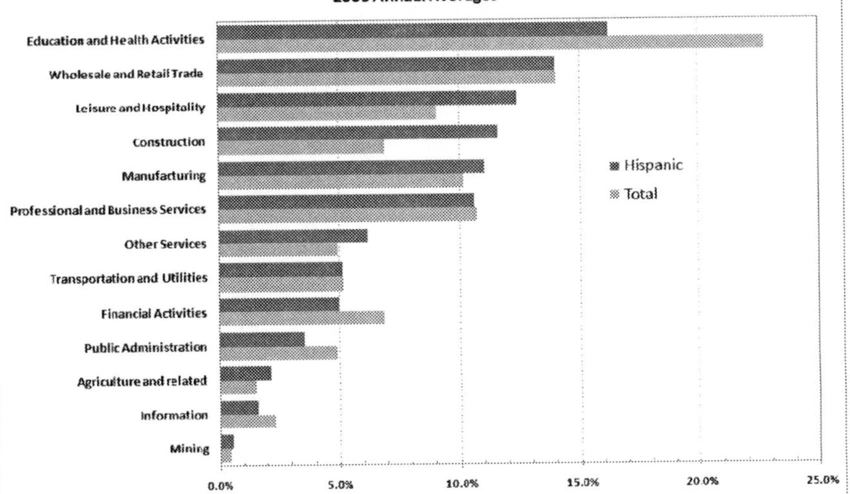

Source: Joint Economic Committee Majority Staff calculations based on data from the Bureau of Labor Statistics.

Furthermore, Hispanic workers have persistently earned a fraction of what the typical worker earns, with median earnings 28 to 31 percent less than those of all employees. Most recently, in the first quarter of 2010, median usual weekly earnings of Hispanic workers were $554, compared to $754 for all workers. This wage gap has made it more difficult for Hispanic workers with a job to accumulate sufficient savings to cushion them in the face of job loss or other financial emergencies.[15]

End Notes

[1] For purposes of the Current Population Survey, Hispanic/Latino/Spanish is considered an ethnicity rather than a racial category. Respondents are asked first if they are of Hispanic, Latino or Spanish ethnicity. In a following question, respondents are asked to identify their race(s) with choices of White, Black or African American, American Indian or Alaska Native, Asian, and Native Hawaiian or Other Pacific Islander. Therefore, respondents who are of Hispanic ethnicity will also be classified separately by race.

[2] State house price declines based on Loan Performance House Price Index for various states, seasonally adjusted by Haver Analytics using X12-ARIMA. Data not available for New Mexico.

[3] Home price declines based on peak to trough dates which vary by state. Housing prices fell 54.5 percent in Nevada from March 2006 to December 2009, 46.3 percent in Arizona from March 2006 to December 2009, 44.8 percent in Florida from April 2006 to December 2009, and 42.9 percent in California from March 2006 to April 2009. In contrast, prices fell 13.3 percent in Texas from the peak in June 2007 to the trough in January 2009.

[4] Loan Performance House Price Index not available for New Mexico. However, the Federal Housing Finance Agency (FHFA) House Price Index for New Mexico shows that the index for New Mexico fell only 6.6 percent from 2007 Q4 to 2009 Q4 compared to an 8.7 percent decline for the United States as a whole. Using the FHFA HPI understates the extent of the housing collapse since it excludes nonprime and jumbo mortgages.

[5] Foreclosure inventory rate, Mortgage Bankers Association, Residential mortgage loans on 1 to 4 unit buildings. Arizona's foreclosure rate rose from 0.5 percent to 6.1 percent, California from 0.8 percent to 5.6 percent, Nevada from 1.2 percent to 9.8 percent, and Florida from 1.0 percent to 13.4 percent. In contrast, the foreclosure rate rose from 1.2 percent to 2.0 percent in Texas and 0.8 percent to 2.99 percent in New Mexico.

[6] Bureau of Labor Statistics, Current Population Survey, Table 2: Median Usual Weekly Earnings, Full-time wage & salary workers by age, race, and sex, quarterly averages.

[7] Bureau of Labor Statistics, Current Population Survey, Table 2: Median Usual Weekly Earnings, Full-time wage & salary workers by age, race, and sex, quarterly averages.

[8] Data are not seasonally adjusted.

[9] Bureau of Labor Statistics, Current Employment Statistics.

[10] Ibid. Construction employment rose in March 2010, for the first time since June 2007, by 15,000 jobs.

[11] State house price declines based on Loan Performance House Price Index for various states, seasonally adjusted by Haver Analytics using X12-ARIMA. Data not available for New Mexico.

[12] House price declines measured from peak to trough. Housing prices fell 54.5 percent in Nevada from March 2006 to December 2009, 46.3 percent in Arizona from March 2006 to December 2009, 44.8 percent in Florida from April 2006 to December 2009, and 42.9

percent in California from March 2006 to April 2009. In contrast, prices fell 13.3 percent in Texas from the peak in June 2007 to the trough in January 2009.

[13] Loan Performance House Price Index not available for New Mexico. However, the Federal Housing Finance Agency (FHFA) House Price Index for New Mexico shows that the index for New Mexico fell only 6.6 percent from 2007 Q4 to 2009 Q4 compared to an 8.7 percent decline for the United States as a whole. Using the FHFA HPI understates the extent of the housing collapse since it excludes nonprime and jumbo mortgages.

[14] Foreclosure inventory rate, Mortgage Bankers Association, Residential mortgage loans on 1 to 4 unit buildings. Arizona's foreclosure rate rose from 0.5 percent to 6.1 percent, California from 0.8 percent to 5.6 percent, Nevada from 1.2 percent to 9.8 percent, and Florida from 1.0 percent to 13.4 percent. In contrast, the foreclosure rate rose from 1.2 percent to 2.0 percent in Texas and 0.8 percent to 2.99 percent in New Mexico.

[15] Bureau of Labor Statistics, Current Population Survey, Table 2: Median usual weekly earnings full-time wage & salary workers by age, race, and sex, quarterly average, not seasonally adjusted in current dollars.

In: Unemployment: A Closer Look
Editors: Jacob S. Mlakar
ISBN: 978-1-61122-762-8

Chapter 10

UNDERSTANDING THE ECONOMY: UNEMPLOYMENT AMONG YOUNG WORKERS

Carolyn B. Maloney

EXECUTIVE SUMMARY

Although the economy has gained strength and overall labor market conditions have improved in recent months, younger workers have continued to struggle finding work. Employers added over half a million jobs in the last four months, yet the unemployment rate for young workers reached a record 19.6 percent in April 2010, the highest level for this age group since the Bureau of Labor Statistics began tracking unemployment in 1947.

Historically, young workers (ages 16 to 24) face considerably higher unemployment rates than prime- age workers (ages 25 to 54). Even before the recession began, one out of every eight young workers was unemployed, a rate of unemployment more than two and a half times that of prime-age workers. While the gap narrowed during the recession, young workers saw their unemployment rate climb steadily and still have a significantly higher unemployment rate than prime-age and older workers.

Specifically, the report shows:

- One-in-five young workers is unemployed – the highest rate of unemployment ever recorded for this age group.

- Young workers make up a disproportionate share of the unemployed. They comprise 13 percent of the labor force, but make up26 percent of the unemployed.
- The youngest workers (16 to17 years) experience the highest rates of unemployment. The unemployment rate for 16 to 17 year olds was 29 percent in April.
- Greater educational attainment reduces the likelihood of being unemployed. College graduates experience the lowest unemployment rate (8.0 percent in April), while those without a high school diploma have the highest unemployment rate (33.0 percent).
- The benefits of a college degree are not uniform among 16 to 24 year olds. The unemployment rate for young black college graduates was 15.8 percent in April, nearly double the 8.0 percent unemployment rate for all young college graduates.
- While young workers face higher unemployment rates than prime-aged workers, young workers typically have shorter unemployment spells. The median duration of unemployment for teens (12.1 weeks) in April was less than half of the median duration among all workers (25.8 weeks). The shorter duration of unemployment may indicate that unemployed younger workers find new jobs more quickly than other unemployed workers, but may also indicate that young workers are stopping their search for work and dropping out of the labor force.
- Young workers are concentrated in sectors of the economy that are particularly sensitive to business cycle fluctuations, such as retail trade and leisure and hospitality. These sectors fared badly during the recession.

Unemployment spells early in a young person's work life can have lasting negative effects on future earnings, productivity, and employment opportunities. It is important, therefore, that policymakers better understand the causes of youth unemployment so that they can act to reduce unemployment among young workers and help them build the skills necessary to regain their footing in the labor market.

BACKGROUND

Historically, unemployment rates have been higher for young workers than for prime-age workers and older workers (55 years and older) [see Figure 1]. Unemployment rates for young workers are more likely to vary counter-cyclically with the business cycle than unemployment rates for other workers because of the nature of their employment – younger workers tend to be employed in temporary positions, are often among the newest employees on the payroll, and are more likely to be employed in "cyclically-sensitive" industries.[1] In the twenty years leading up to the start of the Great Recession, the unemployment rate for 16 to 24 year olds was typically 2.6 times greater than that of the rate for 25 to 54 year olds. In December 2007, the unemployment rate for young workers was 11.8 percent, more than two and a half times the unemployment rate for prime-age workers. Most recently, in April 2010, the unemployment rate for young workers reached 19.6 percent – the highest since the Bureau of Labor Statistics began tracking unemployment in 1947. Although the gap between the prime-age and youth unemployment rates has narrowed during the Great Recession, the large number of experienced prime- age workers looking for work may have worsened the employment prospects of younger workers. For example, the New York Times reported that many college graduates have found employment in jobs that do not require a college degree—jobs that are typically held by younger workers.[2] Currently, five workers are unemployed for every one job opening, which means that competition for work is stiff.[3]

Figure 1. Young Workers Face High Levels of Unemployment
Unemployment Rate by Age, 1974 to 2010 (Seasonally Adjusted)

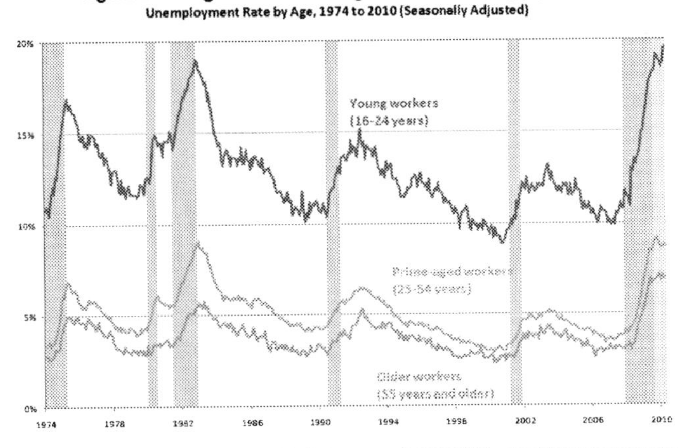

Note: Shaded areas indicate recessions as classified by NBER. Although GDP began to expand in July 2009, NBER has not dated the end of the current recession.
Source: Bureau of Labor Statistics, Household Survey.

UNEMPLOYMENT IS HIGHEST AMONG TEENS

The unemployment rate of young workers decreases with age and educational attainment [see Figure 2]. In general, younger teen workers (16 and 17 year olds) experience the highest rate of unemployment. Their unemployment rate was over 29 percent in April, with nearly one-in-three searching for work. Young teens make up only 1.2 percent of the labor force. The vast majority (93 percent) has no high school diploma, and includes teens that are looking for employment to support themselves or their families. Older teens (18 to 19 year olds) in the labor force are divided among those having no high school diploma (38 percent), a high school diploma with no college (32 percent), and some college (29 percent). The unemployment rate for older teens was 24.1 percent; and they make up 2.6 percent of the labor force. Not surprisingly, young adults (20 to 24 year olds) in the labor market tend to be more educated than teens, with 90 percent having at least a high school diploma, and 15 percent having a 4-year college degree. Young adults constitute almost 10 percent of the labor force (9.8 percent); their unemployment rate was 17.2 percent in April.

Figure 2. Among All Young Workers, Unemployment Is Highest Among Teens

Unemployment Rate by Age, 1974 to 2010 (Seasonally Adjusted)

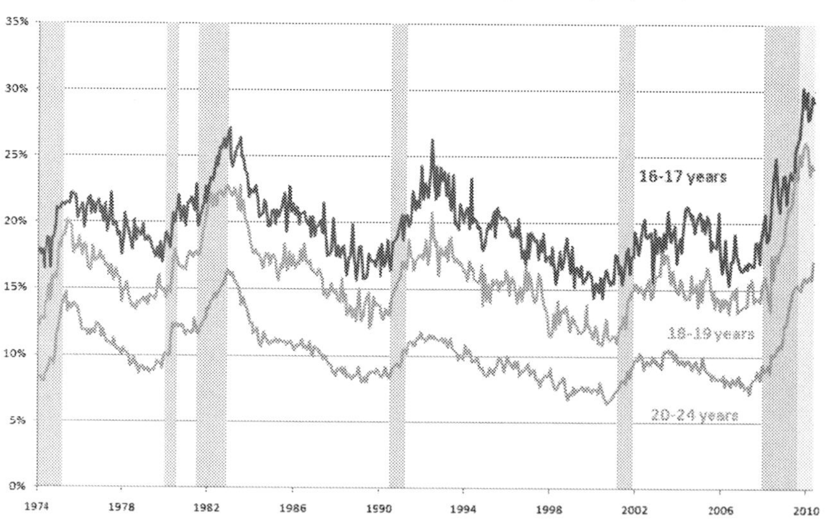

Note: Shaded areas indicate recessions as classified by NBER. Although GDP began to expand in July 2009, NBER has not dated the end of the current recession.
Source: Bureau of Labor Statistics, Household Survey.

EDUCATION IMPROVES EMPLOYMENT PROSPECTS FOR YOUNG WORKERS

Among young workers, greater educational attainment—a high school diploma or some college coursework—can greatly reduce the probability of being unemployed [see Figure 3]. Between April 2007 and April 2010, the unemployment rate for young workers (16 to 24 year olds) with no high school diploma, and not currently enrolled in school, increased from 19.7 percent to 33.0 percent. For young workers with a high school diploma but no college coursework, the unemployment rate increased from 11.4 percent to 24.6 percent over the same period. For young workers with some college but no degree, the unemployment rate rose from 5.0 percent to 14.1 percent. But for those with at least a bachelor's degree, the unemployment rate started out at 3.7 percent before rising to 8.0 percent—1.5 percentage points below the national unemployment rate (9.5 percent in April 2010, not seasonally adjusted). Even for young workers with no college coursework, earning a high school diploma reduced the likelihood of being unemployed from one in three to one in four. Earning a four-year college degree reduced the probability even further, to one in twelve.

Figure 3. Education Improves Employment Prospects for Young Workers

Unemployment Rate of 16-24 Year Olds, by Educational Attainment (Not Seasonally Adjusted)

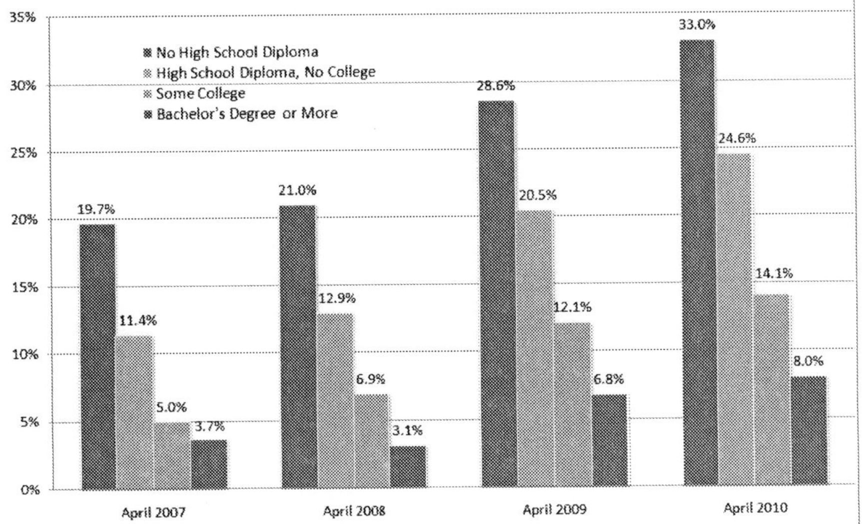

Source: Bureau of Labor Statistics, Household Survey.

Unemployment Is High among Young Minority Workers, Despite Education

Greater educational attainment alone cannot solve the youth unemployment crisis. Even with high levels of education, young minority workers not enrolled in school have distressingly high rates of unemployment. In April, the unemployment rate for young black high school graduates (16 to 24 years old) not enrolled in school was 34.9 percent, compared to 24.6 percent for all young high school graduates not in school. For young black college graduates, the unemployment rate of 15.8 percent was almost double the overall unemployment rate for all young college graduates. While lower than the unemployment rate of 60.0 percent for young black workers with no high school diploma, unemployment rates of 34.9 percent and 15.8 percent are unacceptably high.

Among young Hispanic workers, the unemployment rate for young high school graduates not enrolled in school was 23.2 percent, not statistically different from the overall rate of 24.6 percent. For those with some college, the unemployment rate was 18.9 percent, slightly higher than the overall rate for young workers with some college.[4]

Young Workers Are Disproportionately Concentrated in Industries Hard-Hit by Recession

Young workers comprise 13 percent of all employees, but they are not evenly distributed across industries [see Figure 4]. Young workers are over-represented in leisure and hospitality, where they make up 34 percent of the total workforce, and in wholesale and retail trade, where they make up 20 percent of the total workforce. Both of these sectors have been hard-hit by the recession. Wholesale and retail trade lost 1.68 million jobs since the recession began in December 2007, while leisure and hospitality lost 544,000 over that period.[5] Young workers' disproportionate representation in these fields is likely responsible for some of the difficulties these workers have faced during the slack labor market.[6]

Not only are young workers disproportionately represented in a small group of hard-hit industries, the fact that their employment is so heavily concentrated in those industries may make finding new work difficult.

Examining the distribution of young workers employed across all industries shows that wholesale and retail trade and leisure and hospitality are the primary employers of teens. In fact, two out of every three (64 percent) employed teens (ages 16 to 19) work in one of those two sectors. Young adults (ages 20 to 24) with a job are somewhat more evenly distributed across the different sectors of the economy, with 60 percent of employed young adults working in one of three sectors — leisure and hospitality, education and health services, and wholesale and retail trade. These young adults may be able to move across industries and find new work with greater ease than teenage workers [see Figure 5].

In recent months, leisure and hospitality has been among the sectors showing signs of strong growth. Other expanding sectors include manufacturing, professional and business services, health care employment, and construction. It remains to be seen whether employers in these sectors will hire (or re-hire) unemployed youth. On the one hand, young workers' limited experience may mean that they are less desirable to employers who have begun to hire, especially given the large pool of job seekers that includes many workers with more experience and skills. On the other hand, young workers' limited experience may mean they are less-expensive hires for growing industries, making them "bargain" hires.

Figure 4. Young Workers Are 13 Percent of All Employees But 20% of Wholesale and Retail Trade Employees, and 34% of Leisure and Hospitality Employees

Distribution of Employees by Industry and Age, 2009

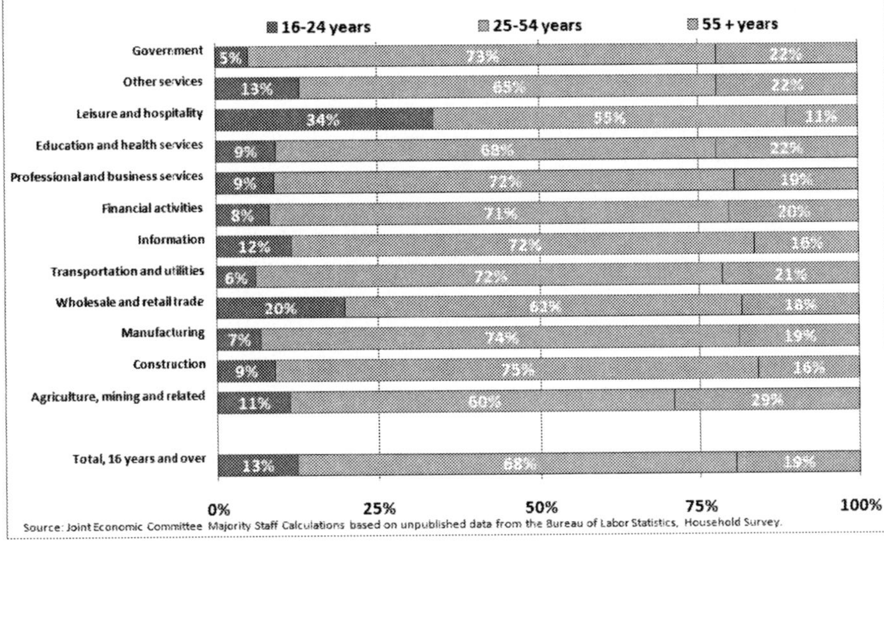

Source: Joint Economic Committee Majority Staff Calculations based on unpublished data from the Bureau of Labor Statistics, Household Survey.

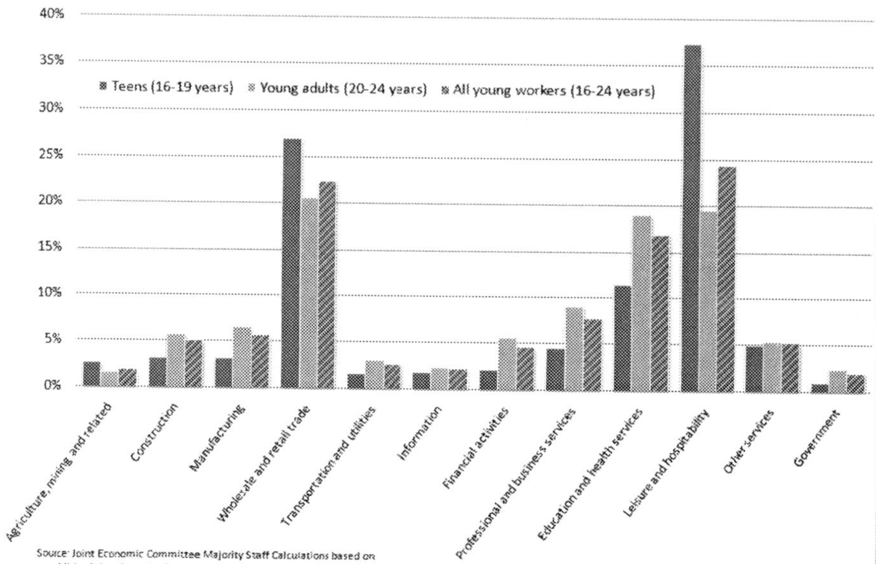

Figure 5. Where Are Young Workers Employed?
Distribution of Young Workers by Industry, 2009

Source: Joint Economic Committee Majority Staff Calculations based on unpublished data from the Bureau of Labor Statistics, Household Survey.

YOUNG WORKERS MAKE UP A DISPROPORTIONATE SHARE OF THE UNEMPLOYED

While young workers make up 13 percent of the labor force, they account for 26 percent of the unemployed (not seasonally adjusted) [see Figure 6]. In other words, one-in-four unemployed persons are between 16 and 24 years old. The greatest disparity is among teens (ages 16 to 19). While teens are only 4 percent of the overall labor force, they make up more than twice as much (9 percent) of the unemployed and 6 percent of the long-term unemployed.

Young workers typically have shorter unemployment spells than prime-aged workers. The median duration of unemployment in April 2010 was 12.1 weeks among teens (ages 16 to 19) and 19.6 weeks among young adults (ages 20 to 24). Among all workers, the median duration was 25.8 weeks. Consequently, young workers make up a smaller share of the long-term unemployed (those out of work for at least 27 weeks) than of the total unemployed population. Twenty percent of the long-term unemployed are between 16 and 24 years old versus 26 percent of the total unemployed.

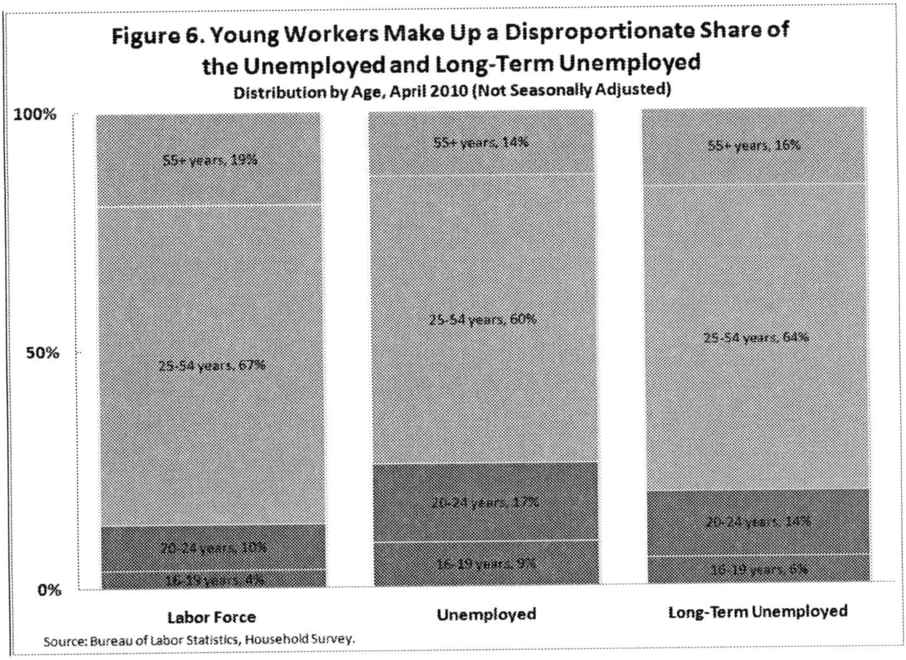

To be counted as unemployed and in the labor force, a person must actively search for work each month. The shorter unemployment spells of younger workers may be indicative of younger workers finding employment. However it may also be the case that younger workers stop searching for work and drop out of the labor force more quickly than older workers. Leaving the labor force to enroll in school can improve a young adult's prospect of finding work later on. However, young workers dropping out of the labor force without enrolling in school is cause for concern.

The labor force participation rate of young workers dropped 3.2 percentage points to 54.2, between April 2007 and April 2010 (not seasonally adjusted). The labor force of young workers shrank by 875,000. However, during the same period, the number of 16 to 24 year olds enrolled in either high school or college increased by 755,000. That increase was greater than the overall increase in the population for that age group, which grew by 602,000 over the same period, suggesting a movement towards enrollment among the younger population. Furthermore, the number of 16 to24 year olds enrolled in school but not in the labor force increased by more than 1.3 million over the same period, and the increase is more than just working students dropping out of the labor force. Subtracting out the change in the number of 16 to 24 year olds in the labor force and enrolled in school (-585,000) and the growth in the overall population of 16 to 24 year olds (+602,000), there were still 153,000 additional enrolled students over the past 3 years.

Data from the Bureau of Labor Statistics confirms that 70 percent of 2009 high school graduates were enrolled in college, up from 68.6 in 2008, and 67.2 percent in 2007. The 2009 level is the highest since BLS began tracking the data in 1959.

While enrollment is clearly up, there remains a group of young workers who have exited the labor force in the past three years. Keeping these young workers attached to the labor market is critical. Young people who give up on searching for work may face significant barriers to entry back into the labor market. As a result, lifetime employment and earnings of these individuals is likely to be significantly depressed.[7] Furthermore, a lack of attachment to the labor market may correlate with a lack of attachment to mainstream values and behaviors, which can in turn lead to problematic behaviors such as crime and delinquency.[8]

HIGH UNEMPLOYMENT CAN HAVE LASTING CONSEQUENCES

The high rates of unemployment among young workers are cause for concern, and the effects can last long after the recession has ended. The "scarring effects" of prolonged unemployment can be devastating over a worker's career. Productivity, earnings and well-being can all suffer. In addition, unemployment can lead to a deterioration of skills and make securing future employment more difficult.[9]

Research shows that young workers entering the labor market during a recession earn less than those who join the labor force during times of economic expansion. Professor Till von Wachter recently testified before the Joint Economic Committee that it may be 10 to 15 years before such a college graduate's earnings catch up to other graduates.[10] For these graduates, the lack of employment opportunities makes paying off student loans a struggle. Graduates in 2008 finished college with an average of roughly $23,000 in student loan debt.

With the economy in recession in 2008 and 2009, student loans increased dramatically. Default rates on student loans also spiked. Demand for student loans has reached record levels, as the recession has forced more college students to take out loans and encouraged more students to stay in school rather than competing for a job in the weak labor market. Outstanding student loans have increased approximately 50 percent since 2007, according to data from the credit bureau Equifax Inc. Student loan defaults have also increased; in 2008, the default rate reached 7.2 percent, the highest level since 1999, and up from 6.7 percent in 2007 and 5.2 percent in 2006, according to the Department of Education.

Action Now Can Mitigate the Harmful Effects of Unemployment

The high unemployment rates faced by teens and younger workers during the recession may call for targeted policies to help these workers find employment and regain their footing in the labor market. Acting now to implement policies that address youth unemployment will minimize the scarring effects for young workers, while benefitting society and the economy as a whole.

In the past four months, the economy has added 573,000 jobs, about the level needed to keep pace with population growth. While this marks significant progress from a year ago, stronger growth will be needed to significantly increase employment among teens and younger workers and to ultimately bring down their unemployment rates.

New graduates will benefit from training programs to ease the transition from school to employment and provide them with skills necessary to succeed in expanding sectors. For youth who have left the education system, programs are needed to keep them attached to the labor force while helping them acquire the skills needed to become, and remain, gainfully employed. Expanding financial aid programs can help young workers ease the financial burden of furthering their education, making higher education more accessible to all young people.

The significant investment in student aid made this spring is particularly timely. The Health Care and Education Affordability Reconciliation Act of 2010, which President Obama signed into law on March 30, 2010, includes the largest investment in student aid in our nation's history. It increases the maximum annual Pell Grant to $5,550 in 2010 and, beginning in 2013, indexes the Pell scholarship to the Consumer Price Index, so that it keeps pace with inflation; channels all new federal lending to the Direct Loan program, saving taxpayers money; invests more than $2.5 billion in historically black colleges and universities and; invests $2 billion in community colleges through a competitive grant program that will help strengthen career training programs.

Beyond investing in financial aid for students, Congress passed the College Cost Reduction and Access Act (H.R. 2669) in 2007 which allowed for income-based repayment of student loans for borrowers experiencing "partial financial hardship."[11] Beginning July 1, 2009, loan repayment for eligible borrowers is capped at 15 percent of their discretionary income, which is reassessed each year. Any outstanding balance would be forgiven after 25 years. As part of the newly-signed health care legislation, Congress and the Obama administration lowered the threshold and maximum payments to 10 percent of a borrower's discretionary income, and shortened the period of repayment before any outstanding balance is forgiven to 20 years. Those changes will apply to new borrowers after July 1, 2014. Additionally, borrowers facing unemployment or other extreme economic hardship can also qualify for a deferment for up to three consecutive years.[12]

In addition, there are several policy actions that could help address the employment challenges facing younger workers.

Job Training – As the labor market strengthens, expanded and improved job training programs may help young workers – workers who have had few prior work experiences – build and rebuild their skills. Better connecting job training to actual placement in a job is an area for potential innovation as is pairing unemployed individuals with corporations for training and employment. Paid internships that expose young people to new occupations and opportunities also offer promise.

Sectoral Employment Programs – Relatively new to the workforce development landscape, these programs work with local employers to build skills necessary for employment in sectors of the local economy where there will be vacancies. Described by Dr. Lawrence Katz in an April 29 JEC hearing, these programs have gotten excellent returns by equipping unemployed workers with skills in demand in their communities. As more communities pursue this approach, particular attention should be paid to ensuring strong participation among younger workers.

Encouraging Mobility Among Young Workers – To recover skills and wages lost during the recession, younger workers will need to be highly mobile across occupation and region. While younger workers are less likely to have mortgages and family obligations that can interfere with moves from one region to the next, they need to be aware of the importance of mobility to getting their careers back on track. Incentives that encourage young people to change occupations, when necessary, and to move to new, faster growing parts of the country could help young workers find jobs and boost their long-term earnings prospects.

Summer Jobs – At the time of publication, Congress was considering the American Jobs and Closing Tax Loopholes Act which would add 300,000 summer jobs for young people. These jobs offer not just wages, but also provide valuable work experience to young people which can lay the groundwork for future employment.

Policymakers must be diligent in examining, understanding and offering innovative solutions to youth unemployment. In doing so, they can avoid a lost generation and instead create the next generation of productive American workers.

End Notes

[1] Stefano Scarpetta, Anne Sonnet and Thomas Manfredi, "Rising Youth Unemployment During the Crisis: How to Prevent Negative Long-Term Consequences on a Generation?" OECD Social, Employment and Migration Papers, No. 106, April 14, 2010 available at http://www.olis.oecd.org/olis/2010doc.nsf/LinkTo/NT000028DE/$FILE/JT03281808.PDF

[2] *New York Times*, "Teenage Jobless Rate Reaches Record High" September 4, 2009.

[3] JOLTS data and number of unemployed persons

[4] The unemployment rate of young Hispanic workers with a 4-year college degree and not enrolled in school is highly influenced by seasonal factors, ranging from a low of 5.2 (April 2010) to a high of 22.8 (December 2009) in the past twelve months.

[5] Employment losses are from start of recession to employment trough. Table B-1. Employees on Nonfarm payrolls by Industry Subsectors and Selected Detail, Bureau of Labor Statistics, Payroll Survey as of April 2010.

[6] Bureau of Labor Statistics, Payroll Survey as of April 2010.

[7] Till von Wachter, Testimony before the Joint Economic Committee, April 29, 2010.

[8] Wilson, William Julius. 1987. *The Truly Disadvantaged*. Chicago: University of Chicago Press; Wilson, William Julius. 1996. *When Work Disappears*. New York: Alfred Knopf.

[9] OECD page 16

[10] Till von Wachter, Testimony before the Joint Economic Committee, April 29, 2010.

[11] Partial financial hardship is defined as having total annual payments on eligible Federal Family Education Loan (FFEL) Program and the William D. Ford Federal Direct Loan (DL) Program loans exceeding 15 percent of their "discretionary" income (adjusted gross income less 150 percent of the applicable poverty line).

[12] See Congressional Research Service Report R41022 by David P. Smole "Federal Student Loans Made Under the Federal Family Education Loan Program and the William D. Ford Federal Direct Loan Program: Terms and Conditions for Borrowers" April 21, 2010

In: Unemployment: A Closer Look
Editors: Jacob S. Mlakar
ISBN: 978-1-61122-762-8

Chapter 11

EXTENDING UNEMPLOYMENT INSURANCE BENEFITS: THE COST OF INACTION FOR DISABLED WORKERS

Carolyn B. Maloney and Charles E. Schumer

The Great Recession left a battered labor market in its wake. The unprecedented rise in longterm unemployment is particularly troubling.[1] Many of the long-term unemployed have continued to receive much-needed support thanks to Congress and the Administration's expansion and extension of the unemployment insurance benefits program. The expiration of the unemployment insurance benefits extension puts millions of out-of-work Americans and their families at risk of real economic hardship. This brief provides an overview of the economic impact of extending unemployment benefits insurance, including a new estimate of the cost of inaction.

Our findings include:

- Unemployment insurance benefits not only provide economic security for individual families. They also boost the nation's economy as a whole. Every dollar spent on unemployment benefits can raise gross domestic product by \$1.60.[2]
- In the absence of unemployment insurance benefits, unemployed disabled workers are likely to drop out of the labor force and turn to Social Security Disability Insurance (SSDI) instead.

- Nearly 290,000 unemployed disabled workers will exhaust their unemployment benefits by the end of 2010 in absence of an extension of the program. The JEC estimates that about two-thirds of these workers will move to SSDI. The cost of shifting these workers out of the labor market and onto the SSDI rolls – *the cost of inaction* – is $24.2 billion.
- In contrast, the cost of providing disabled unemployed workers with extended unemployment insurance benefits and COBRA premium subsidies to facilitate the purchase of health insurance is $721.3 million in 2010.
- The federal government could save $23.5 billion by extending benefits and avoiding a lifetime of SSDI for currently-unemployed disabled workers.

Report by the U.S. Congress Joint Economic Committee Representative Carolyn B. Maloney, Chair Senator Charles E. Schumer, Vice Chairman

Unemployment Benefits Boost the Economy as a Whole

Unemployment insurance benefits are crucial to helping millions of American workers continue to put food on the table and pay the bills. But unemployment benefits also have a significant impact on the strength of the American economy as a whole.

Workers receiving unemployment insurance payments are typically cash-strapped and will spend their benefits quickly. This quick spending generates a "multiplier" for the economy as a whole. Every dollar of unemployment benefits that a recipient spends can generate a cascade of spending by others, providing a significant jolt to the nation's economy. For instance, when an individual spends his unemployment benefits on groceries, the supermarket then spends additional dollars to pay the cashier, the truckers who delivered the food, and the farmers who grew the food. In that sense, every dollar spent on unemployment benefits generates more than a dollar back for the national economy as a whole.

Indeed, the President's Council of Economic Advisers estimates that every dollar spent on unemployment insurance benefits raises gross domestic product (GDP) by $1.60.[3] The non- partisan Congressional Budget Office recently reported that increasing aid to the unemployed is more cost-effective in terms of boosting economic growth and employment than a variety of other policies under consideration.[4]

SPENDING ON UNEMPLOYMENT BENEFITS NOW SAVES ON DISABILITY INSURANCE LATER

831,000 disabled Americans are currently unemployed.[5] The majority of these workers may be eligible for Social Security Disability Insurance (SSDI), which provides monthly payments for disabled workers who are unable to work because of their disability. Enrollment in SSDI is a function of the economic environment because the availability of jobs for disabled workers diminishes in difficult economic times. The extension of unemployment benefits is important for helping keep these disabled workers attached to the labor market, because in the absence of unemployment insurance benefits many of these workers are likely to shift into the disability insurance system.[6] This shift out of the labor market and onto SSDI comes at a substantial cost to the federal government, because once an individual enters the disability rolls, he is unlikely to return to the labor market.[7]

The Joint Economic Committee (JEC) estimates that a failure to extend unemployment insurance benefits would result in nearly 290,000 disabled unemployed workers exhausting unemployment benefits in 2010.[8] The majority, two-thirds, of these disabled exhaustees are likely to turn to the SSDI program for economic support, which means dropping out of the labor market. These SSDI recipients are likely to remain on the rolls until they age off of SSDI and onto traditional old-age Social Security benefits at age 65.[9] This is a costly proposition, especially because SSDI recipients become eligible for Medicare benefits after two years on the disability insurance rolls. *The JEC estimates the lifetime cost of providing disability benefits to individuals pushed out of the labor market by the failure to extend unemployment benefits is over $24.2 billion.*[10]

In contrast, extending unemployment benefits compensation is likely to secure the labor market attachment of these unemployed disabled workers, providing them with the much-needed income necessary to survive in the labor market until conditions improve. In addition, the extension of COBRA premium support, which subsidizes the purchase of health insurance coverage for laid-off workers, provides further key support of particular value for disabled individuals who may have unique health care needs. *The JEC estimates the cost of extending unemployment benefits and COBRA premium support for disabled workers would be approximately $721.3 million in 2010.*[11]

The federal government can spend $721.3 million now on disabled workers, securing their attachment to the labor market for the future. Or it can spend $24.2 billion over the course of these disabled workers' lifetimes on the disability rolls. *Therefore, the JEC estimates that the government can save $23.5 billion by extending unemployment insurance and COBRA premium subsidies today.*

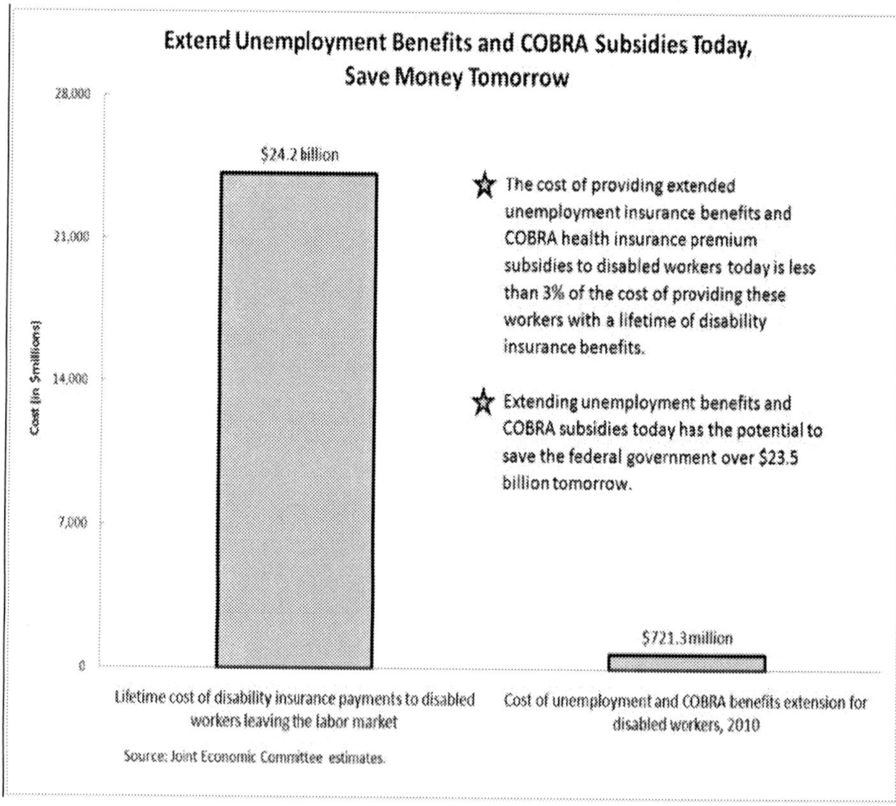

End Notes

[1] See the Bureau of Labor Statistics Household Survey, Table A-12, for data on the duration of unemployment (http://www.bls.gov/ news.release/empsit.t12.htm).

[2] Christina D. Romer, Council of Economic Advisers, Speech for National Association of Business Economists' 25th annual Washington Economic Policy Conference (March 3, 2009) available at http://www.whitehouse.gov/administration/eop/cea/speeches-testimony/03032009/. The Congressional Budget Office estimated that increasing aid to the unemployed would increase GDP from $.70 to $1.90 for every dollar of budgetary cost. See Statement of Douglas W. Elmendorf, Director, Congressional Budget Office, Joint Economic Committee, "Policies for Increasing Economic Growth and Employment in the Short Term," (February 23,2010), available at *http://jec.senate.gov/publi c/index.cfm?p=Hearings&ContentRecordid=dd7e192a-5056-8059-762d-1770c6c35ebf&ContentType* id=14f995b9-dfa5-407a-9d35-56cc7152a7ed&Group id=cb5dcfe4-afee-419f-94eee51eb07de989&MonthDisplay=2&YearDisplay=2010

[3] Statement of Jane Oates, Assistant Secretary for Employment and Training, U.S. Department of Labor, Senate Finance Committee (April 14, 2010).

[4] Congressional Budget Office, *Policies for Increasing Economic Growth and Employment in 2010 and 2011*. January 2010. (http:// www.cbo.gov/ftpdocs/108xx/doc10803/01-14-Employment.pdf).

[5] Unpublished data from the Bureau of Labor Statistics.

[6] See, for example, Stapleton, D., et. al. 1998. "Empirical Analysis of DI and SSI Application and Award Growth." In eds. Rupp, K. and Stapleton, D. *Growth in Disability Benefits: Explanations and Policy Implications*. Kalamazoo, MI: W.E. Upjohn Institute for Employment Research.

[7] Social Security Administration. "Annual Statistical Report of the Social Security Disability Program." Baltimore, MD: SSA, July 2009. (http://www.ssa.gov/policy/docs/statcomps/di asr/).

[8] The JEC utilizes unpublished data from the Department of Labor on the number of individuals exhausting unemployment benefits in CY2010 in the absence of an extension of unemployment benefits combined with unpublished data from the Bureau of Labor Statistics on disabled individuals' unemployment to generate an estimate of the number of disabled workers exhausting benefits in the absence of an extension of unemployment benefits. We assume that share of recipients exhausting unemployment benefits who are disabled is equivalent to the share of the unemployed who are disabled.

[9] Social Security Administration. "Annual Statistical Report of the Social Security Disability Program." Baltimore, MD: SSA, July 2009. (http://www.ssa.gov/policy/docs/statcomps/di asr/).

[10] The JEC utilizes unpublished data from the Bureau of Labor Statistics and unpublished data from the Department of Labor to estimate age-specific numbers of unemployed disabled individuals impacted by the failure to extend unemployment benefits. We then combine those numbers with age-specific estimates of the present discounted value of disability benefits (SSDI plus Medicare) to generate the lifetime cost of disability benefits for these individuals. Estimates for the present discounted value figures come from von Wachter, T. et al. 2010. "Trends in Employment and Earnings of Allowed and Rejected Applications to the Social Security Disability Insurance Program." (*http://www.columbia.edu/~vw2 112/papers/dissa* vwjmjs.pdf). See the web appendix, available at *http://www .columbia.edu/~vw2112/papers/WebAppendixdissa.pdf*. We make two assumptions may result in an upwardly- biased estimate. First, we assume that *all* disabled unemployed individuals are eligible for SSDI, which may not be the case. Second, we assume that none of these disabled individuals would have dropped out of the labor market and received SSDI payments independently of the government's action on unemployment benefits

compensation. We make a third assumption that may result in a downwardly-biased estimate, however. Due to data limitations, our estimate of the cost of SSDI for disabled unemployed workers includes only workers age 35-65. While younger workers are less likely than older workers to enroll in SSDI, our calculations assume the rate of enrollment into will be zero for unemployed disabled workers under age 35. It is reasonable to believe that the rate of enrollment into SSDI for this group of younger unemployed disabled workers will be substantially greater than zero. Therefore, our calculations underestimate the rate of enrollment, which in turn downwardly-biases our estimate of the cost of SSDI in the absence of an extension of unemployment benefits.

[11] The JEC utilizes unpublished data from the Bureau of Labor Statistics on disabled individuals' unemployment to generate an estimate of the share of all unemployed workers who are disabled (5.85%). We assume that the share of total unemployment accounted for by disabled workers is equivalent to the share of the total cost of the unemployment benefits extension that will benefit disabled unemployed workers in order to generate a cost estimate for the cost of the benefit extension to the unemployed. We utilize the Congressional Budget Office score for the cost of the unemployment benefits extension and the COBRA health insurance extension as a guideline for the total cost of the extension.

Chapter Sources

The following chapters have been previously published:

Chapter 1 – This is an edited, excerpted and augmented edition of a United States Congressional Research Service publication, Report Order Code RL33362, dated August 9, 2010.

Chapter 2 – This is an edited, excerpted and augmented edition of a United States Congressional Research Service publication, Report Order Code R41006, dated June 4, 2010.

Chapter 3 – This is an edited, excerpted and augmented edition of a United States Congressional Research Service publication, Report Order Code RS22077, dated April 23, 2010.

Chapter 4 – This is an edited, excerpted and augmented edition of a United States Congressional Research Service publication, Report Order Code RS22440, dated April 22, 2010.

Chapter 5 – This is an edited, excerpted and augmented edition of a United States Congress Joint Economic Committee publication, dated July 2, 2010.

Chapter 6 – This is an edited, excerpted and augmented edition of a United States Congress Joint Economic Committee publication, dated May 2010.

Chapter 7 – This is an edited, excerpted and augmented edition of a United States Congress Joint Economic Committee publication, dated May 28, 2009.

Chapter 8 – This is an edited, excerpted and augmented edition of a United States Congress Joint Economic Committee publication, dated March 2010.

Chapter 9 – This is an edited, excerpted and augmented edition of a United States Congress Joint Economic Committee publication, dated May 2010.

Chapter 10 – This is an edited, excerpted and augmented edition of a United States Congress Joint Economic Committee publication, dated May 2010.

Chapter 11- This is an edited, excerpted and augmented edition of a United States Congress Joint Economic Committee publication, dated May 2010.

INDEX

A

accounting, 55, 60, 67, 69, 71, 72, 77
accuracy, 26
African American women, 110, 113
African Americans, 109, 110, 111, 114, 116, 117, 118, 119, 126
agencies, 3, 18
aggregate demand, 46, 58, 59, 61
airports, 53
Alaska, 9, 14, 24, 83, 134
American Recovery and Reinvestment Act, 2, 8, 13, 16, 34, 38, 40, 42, 44, 50, 65, 69, 100, 105
appropriations, 77
assets, 51, 56, 62, 63, 66
attachment, 6, 89, 102, 146, 153, 154
authorities, 55

B

balance of payments, 67
balanced budget, 59
banks, 51, 65, 90
barriers, 146
barriers to entry, 146
behaviors, 146
bonds, 55
borrowers, 67, 148
budget deficit, 46, 61, 63, 64, 72
budget resolution, 64
buildings, 134, 135
business cycle, ix, 50, 58, 93, 100, 138, 139

C

capital flows, 61, 66
capital gains, 56, 65
capital inflow, 62
cash flow, 64
Census, 106
College Cost Reduction and Access Act, 148
college students, 146
community, ix, 109, 110, 111, 118, 119, 121, 127, 129, 132, 148
compensation, 3, 7, 8, 9, 17, 18, 20, 21, 24, 28, 30, 31, 34, 35, 38, 39, 43, 44, 56, 58, 65, 71, 73, 74, 75, 153, 155
competition, vii, 1, 3, 139
compilation, 83
complement, 57
complexity, 61, 67
compliance, 12, 55
composition, 116
computing, 8
Congressional Budget Office, 63, 67, 90, 92, 153, 154, 155, 156
congressional hearings, 32
cost, x, 43, 46, 49, 51, 52, 54, 55, 56, 58, 60, 61, 63, 64, 84, 87, 90, 98, 151, 152, 153, 154, 155, 156
counsel, 48
crowding out, 61

D

data collection, 11
deficit, 46, 58, 61, 62, 63, 64, 66, 67, 72
delinquency, 146
Department of Defense, 19, 37, 41
Department of Energy, 53
Department of Health and Human Services, 54, 91
disability, 9, 54, 91, 153, 154, 155
disaster, vii, 1, 3, 55
disclosure, 65
discrimination, 52
distortions, 61
District of Columbia, 5, 10, 42, 77, 83
doctors, 54, 56
domestic violence, 9

E

earnings, 5, 7, 8, 11, 12, 29, 31, 70, 77, 80, 95, 96, 97, 98, 126, 134, 135, 138, 146, 149
economic activity, 90
economic crisis, 90
economic downturn, 89, 126
economic growth, 48, 50, 88, 91, 153
economic theory, 50
economic well-being, 100
economy, vii, viii, x, 4, 45, 47, 48, 49, 50, 57, 58, 59, 61, 62, 64, 90, 98, 116, 127, 137, 138, 143, 146, 147, 148, 151, 152
educational attainment, 113, 138, 140, 141, 142
educational services, 54
eligibility criteria, 80
Emergency Economic Stabilization Act, 62
employment, ix, 6, 7, 13, 22, 25, 27, 28, 29, 32, 33, 34, 43, 46, 48, 54, 57, 59, 60, 61, 70, 73, 74, 80, 81, 82, 85, 90, 91, 93, 94, 95, 96, 97, 98, 99, 101, 103, 105, 106, 110, 119, 121, 122, 126, 127, 129, 130, 132, 134, 138, 139, 140, 142, 143, 145, 146, 147, 148, 149, 153
employment growth, 48, 60, 98
employment status, 106
energy efficiency, 45, 47, 52, 57
enforcement, 54
England, 60, 66
enrollment, 145, 146, 155
ethnicity, ix, 106, 121, 123, 132, 134
exclusion, 81
expenditures, 33, 42, 62, 63, 72, 76, 77
experiences, 148
exports, 66

F

farmers, 152
federal funds, 16
federal income tax, 6
federal law, 6, 17, 21, 31
financial crisis, 51, 90
financial market, 50, 51
financial resources, 72
financial sector, vii, viii, 45, 47, 50
financial system, 51
fiscal policy, 50, 57, 58
fluctuations, 4, 138
Ford, 149
foreclosure, 122, 132, 134, 135
foreign banks, 65
foreign capital flows, 61
foreign investment, 65
funding, 3, 4, 30, 32, 36, 46, 47, 52, 53, 56, 57, 69, 71, 77

G

Georgia, 10, 14, 83
Germany, 88
government funds, 80
government securities, 72
graph, 118
Great Depression, 47
gross domestic product, 90, 151, 153
guidance, 31
guidelines, 6, 13, 21, 52, 54, 55, 56

H

Hawaii, 10, 14, 16, 83

health insurance, 54, 55, 57, 152, 153, 156
health services, 122, 130, 143
high school, 138, 140, 141, 142, 145, 146
higher education, 119, 147
Hispanics, 119, 123, 124, 126, 127, 129, 130, 132
historically black colleges and universities, 148
hospitality, 122, 129, 138, 142, 143
housing, ix, 50, 53, 65, 121, 122, 123, 129, 132, 134, 135

I

impacts, 88
income support, vii, 1, 2, 32, 80
income tax, 2, 6, 36, 40, 55, 60, 73
inflation, 147
infrastructure, 45, 47, 51, 52, 53, 57, 59, 64
interest rates, 51, 61, 66, 67
investors, 62

J

job creation, vii, viii, 43, 45, 46, 47, 48, 61, 62, 63, 100, 105, 116
job training, 9, 54, 148
jobless, 48, 87, 89, 90, 100, 103, 105, 113, 116, 117, 124

K

Kentucky, 10, 14, 83

L

labor force, ix, 26, 43, 61, 89, 94, 95, 96, 100, 102, 110, 114, 116, 118, 120, 121, 122, 123, 126, 127, 129, 130, 132, 138, 140, 144, 145, 146, 147, 151
labor force participation, 94, 96, 145
labor markets, 26, 50
landscape, 148
Latinos, ix, 121, 122, 126, 127, 129, 130
law enforcement, 54
layoffs, 31, 32, 57, 88
learning, 54
legislation, 17, 32, 33, 34, 37, 47, 51, 52, 55, 65, 148
legislative proposals, 32
leisure, 122, 129, 138, 142, 143
lending, 13, 49, 90, 147
level of education, 110, 114
lifetime, 146, 152, 153, 155
local government, 36, 45, 46, 47, 51, 57, 58, 59
Louisiana, 10, 14, 30, 83

M

Maine, 10, 14, 83, 85, 86
majority, ix, 90, 93, 140, 153
manufacturing, 55, 95, 116, 122, 127, 129, 130, 143
marriage, 106
married women, 101
means tested, 56
median, 110, 117, 126, 134, 138, 144
Medicaid, 54, 56, 65, 100, 105
Medicare, 51, 52, 55, 56, 57, 77, 153, 155
Mexico, 10, 15, 83, 122, 132, 134, 135
middle class, 51
military, viii, 79, 80, 81, 82, 84, 85, 87
minimum wage, 29
modernization, 14, 34, 42
monetary policy, 58
Montana, 10, 12, 15, 42, 83, 85
multiples, 8
multiplier, 90, 152

N

national debt, 62
natural rate of unemployment, 50
New England, 60, 66
next generation, 149
nursing, 120
nursing home, 120
nutrition, 65, 100, 105

O

Obama, President, 45, 47, 50, 52, 56, 57, 58, 147

Oklahoma, 10, 15, 83
open economy, 58
opportunities, 82, 90, 138, 146, 148
Opportunities, 43, 44, 89
overtime, 61

P

Pacific, 134
pairing, 148
parity, 124
payroll, 4, 16, 54, 56, 59, 70, 71, 139
penalties, 56, 65
pension plans, 56
performance, 48, 50
permission, iv
permit, 34
policy options, 46, 66
population growth, 147
poverty, 52, 54, 55, 56, 87, 91, 149
poverty line, 149
present value, 64
prisons, 120
private investment, 61
probability, 89, 141
productivity, 138
profit, 43
program administration, 5
proposition, 153
public housing, 53
public policy, 31
public service, 52, 53
Puerto Rico, 5, 42, 77

R

race, ix, 106, 109, 111, 123, 132, 134, 135
reasoning, 29, 82
recall, 88
reforms, 34
rehabilitation, 53
renewable energy, 53
resources, 61, 72, 90
retail, 132, 138, 142, 143
retirement, 39, 126
revenue, 4, 13, 16, 17, 51, 54, 56, 59, 63, 72
Roosevelt, Franklin, 42
rural areas, 53

S

savings, 90, 126, 134
scholarship, 147
SEA, 32, 44, 86
seasonal factors, 149
seasonality, 107
Secretary of the Treasury, 73
self-employed, 26, 43, 81, 86
Senate, 32, 37, 43, 44, 46, 47, 51, 52, 54, 55, 56, 57, 64, 92, 155
sensitivity, 88
sex, 106, 111, 134, 135
shortage, 96
short-term interest rate, 51
signs, 143
small businesses, 46, 47, 56, 58
social programs, 87
Social Security, 5, 42, 54, 70, 77, 151, 153, 155
Social Security Disability Insurance, 151, 153, 155
South Dakota, 11, 15, 83, 85
speech, 47, 52, 56
spillover effects, 88
stabilization, 91
state laws, 6, 22, 75, 85
statistics, 100, 119
statute of limitations, 52, 65
stimulus, vii, viii, 3, 6, 7, 8, 16, 18, 20, 24, 28, 29, 30, 33, 34, 35, 36, 44, 45, 46, 47, 49, 50, 52, 55, 56, 57, 58, 59, 62, 64, 66, 69, 71, 88, 91
subsidy, 46, 54, 58, 59, 60, 64
surplus, 4, 72
survey, 60, 64, 66, 106
sustainability, 46, 62

T

TARP, vii, viii, 45, 46, 47, 49, 51, 52, 57, 62, 63, 64, 66, 67
tax cuts, 46, 50, 58, 59, 65, 100, 105

tax evasion, 65
tax incentive, 58
tax increase, 79, 84
tax rates, 65
taxation, 2, 36, 39, 72, 77
technical assistance, 31
teens, 114, 126, 138, 140, 143, 144, 147
Title I, 5, 18, 40, 70
Title II, 5, 70
Title IV, 18, 40
total revenue, 16
trade deficit, 61, 62
training, 9, 31, 34, 54, 132, 147, 148
training programs, 34, 147, 148
transactions, 56, 72, 76
transfer payments, 46, 58, 59
transportation, 52, 53
Treasury Department, 51
triggers, 25, 26, 27, 29, 30, 34
Troubled Asset Relief Program, vii, viii, 45, 47, 49, 65, 67

U

U.S. economy, vii, viii, 45, 50
U.S. Treasury, 16, 18, 24, 35, 69, 71, 77
unemployment insurance, x, 3, 18, 37, 41, 42, 45, 47, 52, 55, 57, 88, 89, 90, 91, 151, 152, 153, 154
United States, 157, 158
universities, 148
updating, 27
urban area, 26
urban areas, 26
USDA, 52

V

vacancies, 148
variations, 26
violence, 9
vouchers, 53
vulnerability, ix, 93, 100

W

wages, 6, 7, 8, 12, 13, 16, 22, 27, 29, 60, 70, 74, 77, 81, 82, 85, 95, 110, 148, 149
West Virginia, 11, 15, 83
Western Europe, 50
White House, 56
wholesale, 132, 142, 143
World War I, 43, 47, 48

Y

young adults, 140, 143, 144
youth unemployment, 138, 139, 142, 147, 149